D0651392

# The Library of Pastoral Care

TITLES ALREADY PUBLISHED

**Sick Call: A Book on the Pastoral Care of the Physically Ill**
Kenneth Child

**Caring for the Elderly**
H. P. Steer

**The Pastoral Care of the Dying**
Norman Autton

**The Pastoral Care of the Bereaved**
Norman Autton

**Casework and Pastoral Care**
Jean Heywood

IN PREPARATION

**Preparing Couples for Marriage**
Martin Parsons

**The Principles and Practice of Pastoral Care**
R. S. Lee

**The Pastoral Care of the Emotionally Distressed**
Chad Varah

**Marriage Guidance**
Kenneth Preston

**Pastoral Care of Children**
Eric Mathieson

**Pastoral Care of Adolescents**
Michael Hare Duke

**The Priest's Work in Hospital**
Norman Autton

**Other volumes are planned**

# CASEWORK AND PASTORAL CARE

# Casework and
# Pastoral Care

JEAN S. HEYWOOD

LONDON

S·P·C·K

1967

*First published in 1967*
*by S.P.C.K.*
*Holy Trinity Church*
*Marylebone Road*
*London, N.W.1*

*Made and printed in Great Britain by*
*William Clowes and Sons, Limited*
*London and Beccles*

TO
THE COMMUNITY OF
THE HOLY NAME

# Contents

# Acknowledgements

Thanks are due to the following for permission to quote from copyright sources:

Russell Sage Foundation, New York: *Toward Public Understanding Casework*, by Viola Paradise.

Routledge & Kegan Paul: *The Last Refuge*, by Peter Townsend.

Gill & Son, Dublin: *Prayers of Life*, by Michael Quoist.

And to the Editor of *Crucible* for permission to reprint parts of Chapter 1, which first appeared as an article "Priests and Social Workers" in March 1964.

# Preface

These chapters are an expansion of seminars I have taken on casework with newly ordained priests and deacons in the Manchester diocese; I have learnt much from the interest and challenge which these clergy brought to the subject. In writing, however, I have been most conscious of what I owe to an old friend, the Reverend F. F. Rigby, Rector of Bromsberrow in Gloucestershire, whose guidance helped me to build the bridge between faith and professional knowledge and understanding. Priests in their parishes are called upon for this bridge-building in both social and personal situations and problems, and I hope that, in some small way, this book may help them.

My thanks are due to Mrs Isabel Makin for her work with the manuscript, and to the Reverend Michael Perry for his editorial counsel.

Part of chapter 1 is from my article "Priests and Social Workers" published in *Crucible* for March 1964, and reprinted here by kind permission of the Editor. I am grateful to the publishers for allowing me to reprint the extracts from their books on pages 33f, 56f, 74.

JEAN S. HEYWOOD

*Department of Social Administration,*
*University of Manchester.*

# 1

## Social Work and its Christian Justification

This book is about the differences and similarities between the pastoral care of the ordained priest and the casework of the social worker. Priests and social workers have a different preparation for their work just because it is different, though the boundaries merge and each needs understanding of the other in order to do his own work properly. In social work there are three main branches. These consist of casework with individuals and families, group work, and community work. In his pastoral care the priest is involved in all three aspects of social work and care. Because of this, he needs more than an elementary understanding of what the social worker does. He needs to understand why the social worker does it. This book will therefore be mainly concerned with the insights of social work as they apply to pastoral care, and understanding of social work functions will have some bearing on the counselling and interpretation which form an indispensable part of all real parish life. Let us then begin by reviewing briefly the various branches of social work and the sort of training that social workers bring to their job.

1. SOCIAL CASEWORKERS help individuals and families who have problems. Central and constant to all casework is the fact of a problem existing. Caseworkers help their clients to see their problem more clearly so that they can make use of the appropriate kind of assistance which the worker can

offer, as he draws all the time on the resources of the social services and gives psychological help. To do this all case-workers use similar skills, but they are employed in different settings, which have their effect on the kinds of problems and people with which they deal and which make the range and scope of their work variable. Casework itself is therefore divided into various branches, which we can look at now.

*Medical social workers,* who were formerly called *almoners,* work in a medical setting; that is, in clinics, public health or welfare departments, and in hospitals. Their rôle is to help patients and their relatives over the social strains and stresses which sometimes accompany illness, so that patients may derive maximum benefit from the hospital or medical treatment they are receiving.

*Probation officers* are attached to courts of justice. They prepare special reports about the offenders when the courts require them and "advise, assist, and befriend" juvenile and adult offenders placed on probation or referred to them for care after a period spent in a custodial setting. They also help husbands and wives who seek advice in matrimonial difficulties and apply to the courts for matrimonial orders.

*Psychiatric social workers* work with psychologists and psychiatrists in hospitals, outpatient clinics, local-authority mental health departments, and child guidance clinics. They are concerned with helping people here who are mentally ill and emotionally disturbed and who come to their setting for psychiatric help.

*Child care officers* work in the children's departments of county and county borough councils and also sometimes in voluntary organizations concerned with the care of children. Their job is to help children who, for various reasons, have to live elsewhere than in their own homes, and they also work with families to prevent the children having to go away from home. They therefore work with both parents and children as a family unit, and also, where appropriate, arrange and supervise fosterings and adoption.

*Welfare officers* are employed by local authorities and

work in welfare services departments or public health departments of county and county borough councils. They are concerned with the aged and physically handicapped and those in the community who need help because of mental disorder or subnormality.

*Moral welfare workers* are the Church's own social workers employed mainly on a diocesan basis. Their concern is for personal, family, and moral problems, particularly of unmarried mothers and illegitimate children and their parents. As part of their work they provide educational opportunities for the preparation of young people for marriage and family life, and to help to increase public awareness of Christian standards and responsibilities in personal and social relationships.

*Family caseworkers* deal with the many different kinds of problem which can arise in family life, but which are not the specific concern of any of the workers listed above. They may work in local voluntary agencies, such as Family Welfare Associations, Personal Service Societies, Invalid Children's Aid Association, and Councils of Social Service, or in some of the Family Service Units which undertake long-term casework with families whose problems appear to be intractable, or whose standards are markedly low. They are increasingly being employed by local authorities in Children's, Health, Welfare, or Housing departments.

2. When we come to look at GROUP WORK we see that the method employed by the group worker is different. Caseworkers have two tools basic to their trade—the relationship between the worker and client, and the interview. The group worker, instead of the interview and client-worker relationship, helps the individual by means of the association he has with others in a group. Group workers are found, therefore, as leaders in youth clubs or adventure playgrounds or as workers in groups which have special personal and social needs—for example, in probation hostels, approved schools, clinics in the mental health field, hospitals, or prisons.

3. THE COMMUNITY WORKER, like the group worker, needs to have a wide range of interests and aptitudes which he can use concentratedly or dilutedly, or spread, like a fan, to meet the needs of the groups; he must have also a particular concern for the development of local community or neighbourhood resources. He is usually employed in a local council of social service, or as the warden of a settlement or community association. Increasingly, community officers are being appointed by local authorities and voluntary organizations to promote the social development of new towns, housing estates, and redevelopment areas in large cities.

For all these jobs social workers need training; the basis of their training is a psychological understanding of people's behaviour and a special understanding of how this is affected by environmental and psychological stress, knowledge of the method by which people with problems can be helped, and knowledge of the social resources available in the community on which they can draw to help people. They have to be experts in these three fields, and it is the integration of these three areas of knowledge which makes their skill. It is therefore a specific skill which may be exercised independently of Christian belief, which does not necessarily form the background of the majority of people who practise it. How then do the priest and the social worker fit in together? This book will attempt to answer this question. First of all, let us begin by asking how social workers and priests see the function of Church and State to-day. Social work is not a secular priesthood, but it is sometimes wrongly interpreted so, and it is not at all unusual to find among priests pessimism and confusion about the whole scope of the Church's work in the welfare state. Traditional compassionate concern for the unhappy and underprivileged, fostered in the past by the Church, and inspiring so many individual men and women to press for humanitarian reforms, is now often said to have become embodied in an impersonal but effective code of legislation, superseding many of the ways of caring which the

Church originated and fostered. Some clergymen are left with a feeling that a good deal of their own work also has been superseded by the social workers of the State, and social workers often do not know where their own boundaries lie.

This uncertainty obscures the truth. We should begin by defining what we mean by the welfare state and by looking at the justification of the concern of both Church and State with the social services. We shall not go wrong if we accept the definition of the social services to-day as our collective provision for meeting social needs in an expanding industrial society.[1] The welfare state with its basis of social service is not something which came into existence in 1948, like Athene springing fully armed from the head of Zeus. It has a long development, traceable in detail at least over the last one hundred and fifty years, and related to the religious and ethical beliefs prevailing in our society at each stage of its growth. One can call some of these beliefs the principle of social obligation, which runs all through Christianity and which provides the justification for Christian social concern. Can we say what this justification is?

Theologians have held that, as God is creator, all created things are his, and man bears a responsibility therefore to God for the right use of them; there is a moral obligation here. But God has done more than just create; because he cares about his creation he has also given guidance about the right use of it. He gave this first in the period recorded in the Old Testament which is about the covenant of God with a *people,* not a city as the Greeks might have imagined it, or a High Priest, as the Egyptians might have liked it, but with a gathered race of men and women trying to understand God, his nature, his purpose, and his will. So the God of the Old Testament made a covenant with the Jews; he promised them certain things if they obeyed his will, and his will consisted of guidance about the right use of his creation. He re-

[1] *The Development of Social Administration:* an Inaugural Lecture by Professor D. V. Donnison, The London School of Economics and Political Science, 1962.

vealed, through Moses, a code of social behaviour relevant to human experience and the whole business of living, concerned with people not just in isolation, or in their secret thoughts, but also interacting one with another. Part of the covenant with the Jews was that they should live their individual lives in the light of this code and relate their civic, social, and political life to it.[1]

This importance of every-day living was later reinforced supremely by what was called the Incarnation. God revealed his nature through Christ in a man. This underlined for all time that humanity—being men—is of supreme concern to God, that man is in relationship to God, and that humanity is capable of revealing insights into God's transcendent nature. By the Incarnation all aspects of humanity have been touched by God. Human life was thus sanctified. He confirmed his concern in his creation—men—in every aspect, and therefore our responsibility for men is also confirmed. The Incarnation underlines that human experience is never a veil, but the *means* to God. Christ, himself, went on to amplify the guidance God had given about this responsibility in ways which men could more easily understand, because they were related to immediate and universal experience. His compassion, comforting, and healing emphasized the importance of involvement in the experience of living, here and now, the material and physical life. His response to living was immediate, before it was cosmic; he healed, but he also made men whole and set them on the road. He did both these things in personal encounter, in which he sometimes also helped men to look at themselves.

So because of this concern with every aspect of humanity, underlined by God in the Incarnation, Christianity has not unjustly been described as the most materialistic of all the great religions. St Paul tells us that Christ proclaimed a new law—that is, he added to the guidance implicit in the covenant—when he told us to bear one another's burdens. This

[1] See the article "A Theology of Social Responsibility" by the Bishop of Colchester in *Crucible*, July, 1962.

law introduces another quality into the code of social behaviour which Christ supremely demonstrated, the strengthening of other people because their need is greater than ours
at the time, letting them borrow or take some of our strength,
even though we have not very much of a surplus, and not
fretting about how much it costs us. Christ demonstrated
this and called it love and said it was an insight into the
nature of God. He allowed men to crucify him, because he
said that life without love was not worthy of the name of life.
It was life without insight into the transcendent nature of
God. Because of this, throughout Christian history, the social
contribution of the Church's members has been demonstrated
in terms of this love or *caritas*. There has been the tradition
that the Gospel and life are meant to supplement each other
and that the Church is therefore concerned with the social
pattern of life and the whole business of human living. The
Church itself has been an instrument of education in the
light of its theology, and this can perhaps most starkly be
seen in the periods of the middle ages, when it exercised decisive social control, teaching against the exploitation of
need implicit in usury, and exacting under penalty of ex-
communication the duty of almsgiving and works of mercy.
In this way a tradition of attitudes was built up which remained effective till the end of the seventeenth century. The
eighteenth and early nineteenth centuries saw a break in this
tradition; cataclysmic social change threw up political doctrines of *laissez-faire*, which were later attacked by a stream
of Christian social thinkers—men so different as Charles
Gore, Henry Scott Holland, Charles Kingsley, F. D. Maurice,
William Temple. These, in their call for social justice—the
right to live rather than to exist—were echoing, in nineteenth-
and twentieth-century terms, the new law of Christ. But
irreparable damage had been done by the application of
political doctrines to the care of those in need—doctrines of
*laissez-faire* and economic expediency about pauperism,
which were in complete contrast to New Testament teaching.
The reconciling of those opposing doctrines on social obliga-

tion was to be the task of Christian social thinkers for the next hundred years.

These first thinkers and teachers were all ordained priests of the Church, but Christian laity have also been concerned, and their protests against the social doctrines of *laissez-faire* were seen in action even before the teachers spoke. Committed Christians demonstrated in specific ways their obedience to Christ's law of comforting and of showing compassion and concern where it was most needed; they worked among under-privileged and inarticulate minorities who were in need and distress, and who could themselves bring no political force or pressure to bear on any government. So we see the work of William Wilberforce for the slaves, Elizabeth Fry for the prisoners, Lord Shaftesbury for cripples, and with Sadler and Oastler for the exploited factory workers, Josephine Butler for the women of the streets, Mary Carpenter for young delinquents, Dr Barnardo for deprived children, Joseph Tuke for the mentally sick, and in our time, the community war-time work of the Society of Friends among families with multifarious social problems, known as the Family Service Units. Except for Lord Shaftesbury's factory reforms, the social services these men and women pioneered were concerned with individual rather than collective distress, and demonstrated social concern for individual conditions of men, roused by human need and human experience and motivated by belief in the value of each individual, whatever his condition, because of his relationship to God. Most of these reformers had wealth and leisure to follow other interests; but it was their religious background which influenced the area of their work and caused them to try to underwrite their social concern into a good society. Their philanthropy illustrates the traditional rôle of the Church in its relation to the social services—a practical demonstration of the giving out of some of their own strengths, spending their money, using their talents and skills, not counting the cost, in the service of those who needed them most, the love

—*caritas*—of the law of the new covenant that Christ made. All this is the ground on which the welfare state was built.

But while this attitude about social obligation has therefore always existed in our society, other factors have influenced the direction it has taken. The old ways were paternalistic; the private philanthropists, or the statutory Poor Law Board were like fathers to their children, providing for their needs in the light of their political or religious doctrines. The political reforms of the nineteenth century, which eventually enfranchised the working population and which were themselves a result of the open-minded freedom to think encouraged by the renaissance movement abetted by religious reformations, brought a new dynamic into the situation; the children began to grow up and to demand some say in influencing the conditions of living and how they were supported or cared for in times of crisis and need. So alongside the philanthropic movement with its work for the underprivileged, we find the democratic movement, itself aiming to reduce the conditions in which poverty, sickness, and ignorance can destroy the quality of life. Men joined together in movements of mutual protection to help themselves in time of difficulty; we find the growth of the co-operatives, trade unions, and friendly societies. These movements paved the way for collective help such as state insurance benefit achieved as a *right,* and not received in charity or pauperism. They are the architects' first draft of the ground plan of the welfare state.

There is yet another crucial factor in the development of the welfare state, one which determined the shape of the building as it were, and that is the establishing of the cause of distress in industrial society. Knowing the cause gives us understanding of how to cure and prevent the distress, and this was the special field of the social scientists at the end of the nineteenth and beginning of the twentieth centuries. The most evident form of distress in industrial society has been the paradox of widespread poverty accompanying increasing wealth and a rising standard of living, and the social scientists set about trying to discover what lay behind this phenomenon. For this they used the inductive method of the scientists. We see this method in the poverty surveys, first of Booth and Rowntree and then of later workers, which examined the living conditions of working people and established the proportion of poverty in representative centres of population, and the conditions responsible for it. These conditions were found to be low wages, unemployment, sickness, and death of the chief wage earner, and proved targets to attack for politicians with a social conscience. The Labour party grew to strength through the trade unions fighting for better wages, and the Liberal government introduced insurance legislation to begin to cover a man's unemployment and inability to work through sickness. So a wedge was driven into the old concept of paternalism, and the people's assertion of their rights to decent living conditions and protection from pauperism, secured by their own financial contribution, became a social objective.

So we see that the ground on which the welfare state is built was prepared by the religious and ethical beliefs which have prevailed in our society, but its building has been a secular political process, and its justification is economic rather than humanitarian, for it is industrial society which provides its *raison d'être*. The social services, for which we all pay by income tax or rates or insurance contributions and which are a form of redistribution of wealth, are required to help individuals to function effectively in a competitive world, to meet our basic needs which cannot be met by a simple, reciprocal agrarian society which no longer exists. So the welfare state is, as described by Lord Beveridge, an attack on those five great corrupting giants of want, disease, ignorance, squalor, and idleness. Poverty and disease are attacked by our system of social security, state insurance, to provide benefits in time of need, family allowances, and our comprehensive health service; squalor and ignorance by successive housing policies and by equality of opportunity up to university level in education; idleness by a planned full-employment policy to which all post-war governments are committed and without which the attack on poverty could not be held. Industrial society needed a medicine for its own disease, and this was the genesis of the welfare state. The welfare state is therefore *an enabling process,* an attempt to eradicate the major disabling social conditions so that the individual can have greater freedom and opportunity to fulfil himself. The social services shape a society which gives the majority of people enabling conditions in which they can fulfil themselves and which is an assertion of their rights as human beings. Such freedom to grow, think, and choose, without the coercion of disabling social conditions, means that people have to become more able to grapple with the complexities of choice; but it also means that self-confidence and self-respect can grow more truly from the exercise of real responsibility. In the welfare state the individual becomes more self-determining; he is called on to make more decisions, he is more, not less, responsible. These things underline the need and value of an education concerned with personal and social responsibility and moral choice. Christian social thinkers would say that society has been or is being altered so that men might live the good life. Perhaps for the first time in our social history we have freedom to try. We are no longer impotent. We have come of age.

But again, one must stress that present society is rooted in industrial competition and economics. Our social services, for all their humanism, can be made to pay only because we are all in work and because our trade and commerce balance in the world markets. The weight of our support is thrown on to those services concerned with keeping us a nation of effective workers—health and education. The cheeseparing of the social services is found in the uneconomic non-productive groups—all services for the aged, the widows, delinquents, vagrants, chronic misfits, and unemployables—those from whom society does not expect a return. Social services here are impoverished and below standard. This is economics, not philosophy or theology. So we talk about "gaps" in the welfare state, and our individual, but not public, social conscience is concerned. Recent concern about this is expressed in all sorts of ways. Perhaps the first well-known statement recently made by the Churches was that of the Council of Christian Churches in Birmingham, which studied the relationships between the social services and the Churches in a suburban area of the city, and which was concerned to find out more clearly what part the Church still has to play in public life and social administration and the formation of policies at central and government level. It was felt that the Church true to its prophetic and educative function has a duty to examine policies and programmes, and that those needs which were unmet in the welfare state were very properly still the field of the Church's compassionate concern. The findings of this Birmingham Social Responsibility Project, as it was called, were published in 1961, and stated that there were five groups of people whose needs were not being properly met:

1. The aged, particularly those incapacitated and living alone.
2. Those suffering from physical disabilities which make normal life impossible or difficult without help or special care.
3. The mentally subnormal and unstable who cannot cope with the pressures of life. (The study did not mention the family's need of understanding support, but this is surely implied.)
4. Social misfits and delinquents of various types.
5. Young people deprived of a satisfactory home background and in danger of becoming delinquent. (Recent legislation in 1963 has gone some way towards dealing with this last category, but it is yet too early to see whether it can be effective without the trained workers.)

These findings show something more than economics at work in the provision of effective social services by the state;

not only are these five groups unproductive and not econo-mically viable, they also arouse strong feelings in all of us. They are concerned with people who have problems which frighten us when we think about them; that is, they rouse our physical horror, or our anxiety that we might become like that, or bring to the surface emotions that we have had to repress; and so we turn away, either by making a moral condemnation or by taking no notice. The feeling reinforces the economics and is more powerful, for it stops us from finding a way through the priorities. If Christian social obli-gation means anything we shall have to begin to look at our-selves and our feelings before we can demonstrate responsi-bility at all. Looking at ourselves demands courage.

It seems then, as we think about the work left for the Church to do in the Welfare State, that there is a primary need for people to become more open to their social responsi-bilities in a way that calls for more imaginative sympathy and more understanding of the dynamics of human be-haviour than we are at present using. It is not just a matter of christianizing social structures; there is a personal growth involved for everyone. There needs to be a climate of opinion which is not so afraid and which is more understanding of the social deviant as a person; while, at the same time not condoning anti-social behaviour, we need to understand the person more. Perhaps we should try to accept more than we do (for this is not socially recognized), that God reveals his grace as much through social failure as through the man or woman who is more manifestly blessed. God uses experience to speak to all of us, but because what he says to us in this way is sometimes hard to take, we do not always listen, and so we lose the immediacy of our lesson and all to which it can lead us. So perhaps there is an even more special job for the Church to do through its historic social rôle in helping society to understand the *nature* of human stress and how people *feel* when they are caught up in crisis situations. Greater un-derstanding in society can create more communities willing to put aside some of their fears and *feel* into the problem of their neighbour, so that they can comfort him and show concern for him. The Church must be concerned, as Christ was, with the business of living, with problems of evil and suffering as they are manifested in each, and more informed awareness is needed of how we can strengthen each other's capacity either to bear or to cope with them. We do not have to wait for complicated problems which require professional help. They are already all around us as part of each developing stage in life, and there is lamentable insensitivity and ignorance about them; the struggle of the adolescent, for example, to come to terms with authority, his ambivalence about independence, his need to throw off childhood inhibitions and to channel resurgent instincts into socially acceptable ways which do not destroy his own individuality; the struggle against renunciation or with changing personality which must be faced in late middle age; the desolation of the elderly, bewildered by their changed bodies and their fear of losing mastery over themselves. Until we have faced with people what these things really mean to them, we do not understand the meaning of life's experience, and neither they nor we can live life abundantly nor have insight into the meaning of God. So the Church, because of its committal to man, is needed to help us all not to push our problems away in an atmosphere of continual euphoria, but to face them and to overcome the discomfort and fear which facing them creates in us. Only in this way can we really free ourselves to love and help the people who need us before living is possible for them. This calls for an attitude of mind as well as an act of will.

What does all this mean in relation to the theology of the welfare state? In the past the begetter of social conscience has been the Church. It has roused public conscience and been concerned to alter society in order that men might live the good life, and has demonstrated its concern in social thinking and philanthropic works. Nonetheless, the welfare state is really a secular thing, brought into existence by the assertion of democratic movements and the studies of the social scientists. To-day it is man who needs to grow before we can alter society any further, and growth means enlargement of our understanding of human experience, understanding each other, acceptance of each other's difficulties, insight unclouded by fear or hate, and enlarged by courage and sensitivity. This means using the knowledge that has come to us from many fields, psychology and sociology, as much as the insights of our faith. It is dependent, first of all, upon self-knowledge and self-discipline.

There is some evidence that this concern is beginning and that it is involving communities, not isolated reformers. Up and down the country small groups are being formed, enlisting voluntary helpers to give neighbourly help to the aged, families of mentally handicapped children, and isolated disabled. Some of them, like the Samaritan groups, have training programmes in which the participants learn not only about the social conditions, but about behaviour under stress and how to reach out to the person in trouble. They aim to give understanding and show concern, both of which will strengthen the person to cope at the first sign of difficulty, or they try to enable the person to accept help from professional social workers if the problem is too big. At the same time the Church Assembly Board for Social Responsibility issues a journal[1] in which contemporary social and psychological problems are being much more openly explored. Papers and books on such topics as suicide, abortion, sterilization, homosexuality, psychology of middle age, etc., are being produced. The priest must learn about human nature in order that he can know how to make theology relevant to it. The insights of contemporary psychology and contemporary sociology show that the theology has to be reinterpreted in contemporary terms. We ask not only what God means in the light of redemption and atonement, but what he means to man's experience of feeling and doing. Again, the rationale of moral values has to be restated in

---

[1] *Crucible*; published six times a year.

terms which have meaning—a difficult task but one which the Church, in its teaching function, cannot escape.

This growth of concern and understanding for *feeling* man has to be more than a willing conscious attempt to do something. It calls for a new attitude, an admitting awareness, in ourselves as well as others, of the weaknesses inherent in human nature, of evil and suffering, and of the struggle to make of them something different. This could be the new theology of the welfare state. It is surely the theology of the New Testament. We shall be looking at this again. Love here is primary: we need knowledge, discipline, and self-awareness to strengthen other people in trouble and to be clear-sighted ourselves. How do we strengthen other people? In contemporary terms the welfare state makes us ask—what is the Cross, and what is the good news?

# 2

## The State and Human Need

Human beings have certain needs, basically the same for all of us, which make it possible to plan the mass programmes we have for the public social services. Such things as adequate food, shelter, and clothing, affection, a feeling of accomplishment, social contact, and the security of law and order are always needed, and are the objectives of the good society. But while men are basically similar, they are also individually unique and different, and people's response to each fresh experience is compounded out of their individual constitutional endowment and earlier life experiences up to that point. We carry potential for our own individual growth and development in our personality, which can be strengthened by good experiences or warped by bad ones. This underlines the importance of environmental influences and all interacting experience. Some bad experiences cannot be totally legislated away; death, accident, disappointment, and failure happen to everyone. According to our endowment we try to cope with them. Eventually, if a man has too many bad experiences, his capacity to deal with them deteriorates; he needs help to cope; if he does not get it he may eventually break down. Some single experiences in themselves can strain people to breaking-point.

This is where the social worker can often help. Behind each social worker are the resources of the welfare state, the public and voluntary social services, which are built round recurring problems. The main public services are concerned with predominating human needs—the five great evils of poverty, ignorance, unemployment, sickness, and the squalor of bad housing and slum conditions. We can look now at the public social services and see how they attempt to meet both mass needs and individual differences at the same time, a rather difficult task.

The most fundamental human need is the provision of means to live, the conquest of poverty. Various surveys have been made in the past to find out the causes of poverty in order that it may be eradicated; the main cause was found to be the lack of relation of income to size of family, and behind this lay social problems of unemployment, low wages, or death or illness of the chief wage earner. To eradicate poverty, therefore, a national policy was needed at government level to ensure full employment, raise the wages of the lowest paid workers and provide a health service where all may have access to the best medical attention at both the preventive and curative stages. It can therefore be seen that the two services most fundamental in attacking poverty are health and education, and bound up with this provision must come a guarantee of full employment and a living wage for everyone.

The National Health Service is therefore available to everyone in the country, irrespective of nationality, age, income, or insurance qualifications. Within the National Health Service are various branches. The hospital and specialist branch provides free treatment on a regional basis, as far as possible associated with a university having a school of medicine, so that similar high standards prevail throughout the country. The services of a medical practitioner are also available free to everyone in the country, and the doctors have facilities for referring their patients, children or adults, where necessary, to the specialist doctors attached to hospitals, and for supplying needed drugs, medicines, and appliances without charge. Similarly, the general services of a dentist and ophthalmic optician are available to everyone, though here most adults pay a charge for part of the cost of treatment. These branches may be regarded as the curative branches of the National Health Service and are largely under the control of the regional hospital boards, hospital management committees, and local executive councils.

Child Guidance clinics also are established to help parents and their children with difficulties in behaviour or family relationships. They may be administered through hospital management committees or local education authorities, though a few voluntarily supported clinics still exist. Their treatment involves work by a team consisting of a psychiatrist, educational psychologist, and psychiatric social worker.

The preventive side of the health service is carried out through the local authorities, the county, county borough, and London borough councils, which are required to provide a local health service, whose executive officer is the local Medical Officer of Health. This service consists of the provision of health centres; arrangements for the care of expectant and nursing mothers and children under five years of age who are not attending school and who are therefore not covered by the school health service; a midwifery service; a full health visitor service; a home nursing service; an ambulance service; arrangements for the prevention of illness and care and after-care of the sick; a domestic help scheme; a vaccination and diphtheria immunization service; the supervision of mentally subnormal people living in the community, and the community care of patients suffering and recovering from mental illness.

The health visitor is the front line of the preventive service. She is a state registered nurse, specially trained to visit people in their own homes in order to give guidance on the care of young people, expectant and nursing mothers, the elderly, persons suffering from illness including mental illness, injury, and disability, and to give advice about the prevention of the spread of infection. She has a crucial and important rôle to play as the first helper and guider in the preventive health field. Special concern is also shown through the health service for illegitimate children, since babies in the first year of life are specially vulnerable to poor environmental conditions, and the infantile mortality rate of illegitimate babies used to be very high. Most local authorities therefore give financial support and use the voluntary moral welfare associations of the Church, whose workers give help with their problems to those unmarried mothers who need it. Moral welfare workers—who are social workers—and health visitors—who are health workers—have to work together here with what are often interwoven problems of health and personal and social factors. As a result of this co-operation the infantile death rate among illegitimate babies now shows little variation from that of legitimate babies.

Local health authorities may also employ Home Helps to be used to provide domestic help in the home where it is needed because of sickness, old age, maternity, or the welfare of children. They are employed and paid by the public health committe who may recover a reasonable charge from the householder if they consider he can afford to pay. The help may vary from full-time, including night attendance, to a few hours a week, dependent on the person's need.

The mental health services of the local authority try to provide special services within the community for mentally disordered patients who do not require hospital treatment. These special services include the provision of centres for the training and occupation of mentally disordered people and local residential accommodation for those who need it. Trained mental welfare officers are appointed to help with the provision of services and to exercise the care and visiting required when persons have to be placed under guardianship.

The system of public education is designed to give maximum educational facilities to everyone without cost. It is organized into primary full-time education for pupils below the age of twelve, secondary full-time education for pupils over twelve and under nineteen, further education, which may be full- or part-time education, for persons over compulsory school-leaving age, and provision for recreation and social and physical training. Local education authorities are fully responsible for primary and secondary education in county schools in their own areas and bear a share of the responsibility for the voluntary schools. Two further classes of school, known as direct-grant schools and independent schools, are outside the direct management of the local education authority. In making educational provision the local authorities are required to have regard to things other than pure education, and to provide for some social needs as well. Hence they can provide nursery schools and classes for children under five years of age and special day or residential education for certain handicapped children, such as the blind, partially sighted, deaf, partially hearing, delicate, educationally sub-normal, epileptic, maladjusted, physically handicapped, and those suffering from speech defects. The local education committee must provide a school health service, provide milk and meals for pupils in schools maintained by them, and see that the laws regulating the part-time employment of children are adhered to.

The educational services are helped by the Ministry of Labour to advise young people about careers and employment before they leave school. Local offices of the youth employment services are available to all school leavers up to the age of eighteen; they may be staffed by officers of the Ministry, and the Ministry may appoint the committee, or local education authorities may operate the service themselves. Young people are helped by the youth employment officers to find employment suited to their aptitudes and abilities, and the officers, who have received special training for their work, follow up and keep in touch with young people during the early years of their working lives.

So the two primary services of health and education prepare and maintain people to be fit and able for a working life where full employment can be guaranteed. Without full employment the welfare state would crumble, so that national policy must be concerned with the economics of work and industrial relations. As part of this concern, the first labour exchanges were opened as long ago as 1910 and administered by the Board of Trade. There is now a network of employment exchanges throughout the country, for which the Ministry of Labour is responsible. The main purpose of the exchanges is to bring together the employer wanting workers and the workman seeking work or a change of employment, the officials of the Ministry of Labour at the exchanges using their knowledge about individual conditions of employment and trade to help both sides. Disabled persons are also registered at the exchanges, and helped to find suitable employment and, where appropriate, arrangements are made for vocational training or industrial rehabilitation so that suitable employment in a skilled trade can be obtained and shortage of labour in industries of national importance can be made good. The exchanges also operate transfer schemes to help persons to undertake work in other parts of the country if they cannot use their skill locally, and special arrangements can be made for persons who are seriously disabled and able to work only under special conditions. Special Disablement Resettlement Officers at the Employment Exchanges are concerned with the problems of work for disabled people.

Meanwhile, the Ministry of Labour itself gives advice and help for the improvement of industrial relations and may arrange arbitration for the settlement of industrial disputes. In some industries, conditions of employment and minimum wages are statutorily regulated and enforced by Wages Inspectors, but in most forms of employment there is no such enforcement. Instead, Industrial Relations Officers, stationed at the Ministry's regional centres, not employment exchanges, are able to give advice about the conditions and terms of employment which have been fixed through voluntary agreements between employers and trade unions. In factories and workshops conditions of work are maintained at a statutorily approved standard by the Ministry's factory inspectors.

With the provision of services for health, education, and

work, some major basic needs are being met, but, as a safe-guard, some assurance is needed against loss of income through temporary sickness or unemployment. This concept lay behind the comprehensive system of insurance recommended by the late Lord (then Sir William) Beveridge in his Report on Social Insurance and Allied Services, published in 1942, and later embodied in the National Insurance Act of 1946. Under this Act insurance is compulsory and, with a few minor exceptions, covers all persons in Great Britain over school-leaving age and under pensionable age, who are required to pay contributions weekly to insure themselves for payment at times when their capacity to work is impaired; the benefits are therefore payable during unemployment, sickness, maternity, retirement, widowhood, and they include guardians' allowances and a death grant. The benefits are related also to family size in that they include allowances for children. This principle of attempting to relate income to family size was applied also to all working people through the payment generally of family allowances.

The important status of workers was underlined in 1946 by the repeal of the old workmen's compensation acts and the substitution of compulsory insurance against death or injury by accident arising out of and in the course of a person's employment. Such disablement is now dealt with on lines analogous to injury in the armed forces and so symbolizes the important rôle the worker plays in the welfare state in defending its very existence.

Supplementary benefits are intended to ensure that no-one, through any circumstances which are not covered by insurance or other means, should be left in poverty below subsistence level. In 1966 the old Ministry of Pensions and National Insurance and the National Assistance Board were replaced by a comprehensive Ministry of Social Security. The new ministry deals with national insurance, war pensions, and family allowances, and has taken over from the old National Assistance Board the administration of noncontributory and supplementary benefits. Financial assistance may be given in the form of supplementary benefits to anyone over sixteen years of age who is not in full-time work (other than individuals involved in a trade dispute, whose dependants only then qualify). Applications for help are made to the local area office of the Ministry of Social Security. Those who are under pensionable age and available for work apply for help through their local employment exchange. Others can get a form of application from the Post Office and, when it is filled in, it may be taken or posted to the local office of the Ministry. The Ministry's officer then calls to obtain particulars of the circumstances of the applicant and to assess his need of the help which he can now claim from the Ministry.

There are also other crucial periods of need when families are most often wanting help; that is, when children are small or adolescent, or when members are old. There are three separate services which deal with needs here. For families who are experiencing difficulties with their children there is the child care service, administered by social workers through the county councils and county borough councils, whose chief officer is known as the Children's Officer. They work to help families in their homes and to resolve the problems there, but if this is impossible they have powers to receive or even remove children into care and bring them up in an atmosphere of affection and security in a specially chosen foster home or some form of residential care. A similar service is operated for the elderly and adult homeless, through the welfare services departments of county councils and county borough councils, and various forms of residential care are provided. Probation officers deal with the needs of those families where there are delinquents who have been before the court and found guilty of an offence, and help those who are released from custodial care. At the time of writing there is a distinct possibility that these three services may be merged together in a comprehensive casework service provided through the local authorities, aiming to give a case-work service to all who are in need of it. The parish priest needs to know all these services and how they are developing, so that he can use them in his ministry.

On the face of it, it would seem that the major common human needs are met, structurally at any rate, by an organization of social services operating at key situations in the life cycle. But human nature is not as simple as that. Besides the social situation we must see the dynamic human situation, what the individual personally makes of his circumstances. This will differ for each man, woman, or child according to his personality, history, experience, and the stage of development in which he is. The framework of the services may be constructive, good, and helpful, but it may not always be enough for a particular individual.

So within the mass programme of social services, there has to be a body of workers who are able to help people when a problem becomes more than they can manage alone. We call the social workers "caseworkers" because they are concerned not only with general social problems but with a specific case situation made up of the individual, his circumstances, his family, his experience, and his response to his situation. Examples of caseworkers are the medical social worker in the hospital, the psychiatric social worker in the child guidance clinic, and the workers for families, delinquents, and elderly persons in the child care, probation, and welfare services. They are concerned with the specific rather than the general, the unique rather than the common denominator; they are working always with a personal problem, usually some psychological stress which is affecting a person's ability to cope with his circumstances and to fulfil himself in society. The social caseworker therefore has the double function of bearing a responsibility to help his client in his needs, but also a responsibility to society to see that he does not injure society in doing so. He is a *social* caseworker, standing for the values of society, as well as understanding the compulsion of basic human needs, and he is subjected to the cultural influences of the society in which he works. Another part of the responsibility arising from his professional knowledge and professional experience is to bring his influence to bear in trying to change and modify society in order to make it better, but his view of what is better will in the end depend upon his own and society's moral values, and he cannot be too far removed from the majority of people if they are to listen to him at all. To take a very blatant example, a worker from a Christianized western European society will have some added difficulty in deciding how best to advise clients in a different social culture—in North America, for example, about divorce, in old Japan about honour and suicide, in the Soviet Union about freedom of enterprise. The social culture, itself related to moral and ethical concepts, conditions the choices the worker can put before his client as a solution to his problem. The culture is surely a ground for dialogue between the caseworker and priest.

The connection between the social culture and the social worker is very important and crucial. The social caseworker is not a professional expert in the field of absolute morality in the way that the priest is. He is concerned with a job which is a step removed from this, the response of a unique individual to a situation which creates a problem compounded of personal factors and social circumstances. The social element therefore must always be taken into account. The administration of the social services in which the caseworker works ensures that this is done because of the public accountability imposed.

On the next page is a table showing the statutory social services in which most of the social caseworkers work. Some notes explaining what the workers do were given at the beginning of the first chapter. It will be seen that each agency has a different function, and also that it has a different *structure*. The power lies with different groups of people. In some services—child care, for example—there is a complicated legislation which has to be operated, and for whose

27

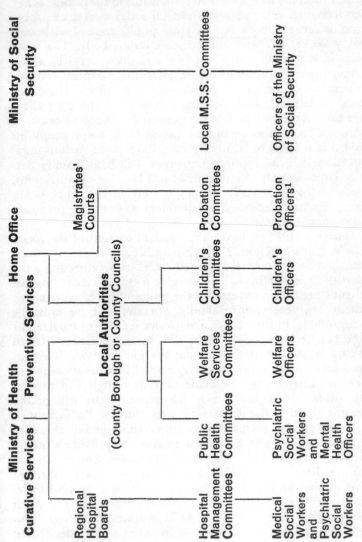

| Ministry of Health | | Home Office | | Ministry of Social Security |
| Curative Services | Preventive Services | | | |
| | Local Authorities (County Borough or County Councils) | | Magistrates' Courts | |
| Regional Hospital Boards | | | | Local M.S.S. Committees |
| Hospital Management Committees | Public Health Committees | Welfare Services Committees | Children's Committees | Probation Committees | |
| Medical Social Workers and Psychiatric Social Workers | Psychiatric Social Workers and Mental Health Officers | Welfare Officers | Children's Officers | Probation Officers[1] | Officers of the Ministry of Social Security |

1 Salaries paid by local authorities.

application the worker is held responsible to the public; other services, such as those of the medical social worker or probation officer, are more remote from public control, although every worker is answerable to some public body. The table shows the structure of power of the statutory services which employ caseworkers. Power is exercised by financial control, which is dictated by lay people—members of Parliament or local councillors, and the men and women who elect them are the people who provide the money for the services either through local rates or income tax or both. Some people in addition will make voluntary contributions to various organizations which employ caseworkers—such as Family Service Units, Family Welfare, or Moral Welfare organizations, because they believe in the importance of this work being done in a particular and independent way and are prepared to support it financially.

These points emphasize the "social" content of the social caseworker's function. He is responsible to the society which has approved his service. The caseworker therefore has a tripartite responsibility—he must give a service centred on his client's need, he must respect the policy of his lay committee about how the service should operate, and he must be accountable, in the case of a statutory service, to Parliament and people for what he does. This responsibility is secured by the legislation defining what the social service is about, and making the local authority responsible for its administration. Changes can be made only by bringing in new or amending old legislation, which expresses the will of the people through the democratic procedure of Parliament.

The caseworker therefore cannot run too far ahead of public opinion, and he has three aims: to provide a public service within a legal framework; to assess the *entitlement* of the client to the service and, when this is established, to ensure that he is enabled to make full use of it; and to reconcile the needs of the client with the sort of service which the public meant to provide. As he operates the service, however, the caseworker often finds impasses and inadequacies;

his professional knowledge, which is always being extended, is greater than that of the lay administrator or public legislators and enables him to see how the purpose of the legislation could be better served in other ways. He has therefore to feed some of his knowledge and understanding back to the public if things are to improve. The social caseworker has an educative rôle in society as well as a helping rôle with clients. His educative rôle arises out of his experience of working with people in need and his concept of what the good society means. Unless the priest and social worker thrash this out together there is a possibility that different standards of good may emerge. Therefore, in carrying out his job the caseworker has often to bring pressures to bear on lay people to get legislation altered. He does this through his impact on his lay executive committees, which usually consist of local influential persons, and by making known the difficulties of operation to the central government inspectorate. This is fairly standard procedure in the fields of child care and probation, for example, and some amending legislation has already been brought about this way. Other caseworkers, such as medical and psychiatric social workers, do not have the same sort of structure within which to work and therefore have to rely much more on presenting facts to the relevant government departments through their professional associations, and pressing for changes in the legislation this way.

It is, however, a rather sobering fact to see how slowly the public responds to this professional sort of guidance. The kind of problem with which the caseworker deals is not in the front of most people's minds. There is in fact no person in the world who does not at some time or other have a personal problem which could be solved by casework help, but the general social pattern is not to go to a caseworker. We struggle on, concealing it, or getting help from friends, relatives, or wise acquaintances, or perhaps a personal problem page in a magazine or newspaper. Much of this advice is very good and sound and is quite sufficient to help a number of people to cope with their situation, but often it is not. It may be compared to the general advice, based on general knowledge about health which is prevalent among the population. It is very sound as a general rule, but when people are sick it is not enough. Their bodies do not respond to a general rule; they need something more specific. What exactly they need will depend upon what is the matter with them. Therefore, the most important thing which the doctor has to do is to establish a diagnosis for each individual case.

In his own field this is what the social caseworker has to do, but instead of the diagnosis being medical it is psychosocial. That is, it takes into account the psychological and social factors which have caused the problem.

Most of us are rather quiet about the psychological and social factors in our lives. We are taught to paddle our own canoe, to keep up appearances, not to wear our hearts on our sleeves. This is why casework did not develop in this country among "the middle class". It developed among the poor whose environment was so appalling, and resultant psychological and social problems were so great that they could not be covered up; they intruded into the pattern of living of other people, public assistance was overwhelmed, hospital care was rendered ineffective by home conditions and had constantly to be repeated; school learning was impeded; crimes of violence increased; children were neglected or abandoned. These are the areas in which the public thought it worth while to appoint social services with caseworkers to deal with what is distressing, and this is still very largely the pattern to-day. Casework is still usually associated in the public mind with the people's underprivilege and nuisance value. Very little propaganda has ever been put out about what casework can do (partly because we have never had enough practitioners strategically placed), and perhaps even the majority of local government councillors believe it is a method used for helping weak, anti-social personalities to become respectable and socially conforming. The conception of the caseworker as someone working with the healthy, adaptive part of the personality, strengthening rather than changing adaptive processes, using great diagnostic skill in treatment, is too new to be widely understood or accepted, and caseworkers are still largely concerned with clients drawn from lower income groups. The more general public impression of what caseworkers do is reflected in the frequent passing of legislation before sufficient personnel have been trained to operate it. The legislation therefore remains largely ineffective, but it absolves the public conscience and points to the direction in which the social services should go.

It may therefore be of interest now to compare what is the position elsewhere, in North America, for example, where casework is much more "respectable" and much more widely used among a greater variety of people. Casework in the United States, as here, began inside the voluntary organizations but has largely remained with them, and this seems to have had an important influence on the use which has been made of caseworkers there. From the nineteenth century onwards workers themselves have always realized that many human problems, though accentuated by poverty, exist irrespective of financial conditions. Under similar economic circumstances one family would go under, another continue somehow to get along. Environmental conditions were not the only factor in the problem, important as these were, and it was in North America in the twenties, under the impact of the new understanding from dynamic psychology, that caseworkers began to study the forces inside the personality which allowed deterioration in some and resisted it in others. Although the main problem with which they worked had a financial origin, they learned to work with an understanding of the personality, which transcended this and was relevant to both psychological and social problems, independent of economic conditions; and this was a crucial step in the development of casework, which became centred round personality conflict.

In the depression of the thirties the responsibility for the relief of poverty was placed in the United States, as here, on the public social services, and caseworkers in the voluntary agencies who had largely been concerned with the poor were now challenged—what was there for them to do? There was practically no public awareness of the added skills they had acquired and they were put on the defensive. The position was intensified during the last war when America experienced full employment, and poverty diminished—but this time the rôle of the caseworker began to come clear. The emotional problems thrown up by the war were very widespread and openly acknowledged. Driven by these emotional pressures people in quite well-off financial circumstances began to bring their troubles to voluntary agencies, where most of the caseworkers were: mothers, bewildered and frightened by the absence of their husbands and by their children growing up without a father; disturbed adolescents groping for their niche; men confused and mortified by their rejection or discharge from the armed forces before the war had ended. As the caseworkers used the knowledge taken from dynamic psychology they were able to deal effectively and began to attract a more representative clientele. As a result, during the war some fifteen member agencies of the Family Service Association of America established fee-paying services for those who could afford to pay, and this gave respect and status to the clients who made use of the casework. Although the pattern was not followed everywhere it did much to establish the value and effectiveness of casework, since people would not pay for an ineffective service. The skill of the caseworker in diagnosing the problem and offering appropriate help became crucial to the use and development of their services.

As their skill increased, the workers felt that the people who needed it had a right to the special help which casework could give and that there was need for more public information about it. During the 1950s the following statement was published by the Cleveland Family Service Association of Cleveland, Ohio.[1]

[1] Viola Paradise, *Toward Public Understanding of Casework*, Russell Sage Foundation, New York, 1958, pp. 89–91.

## Casework—what is it?

Casework is a profession which helps a troubled person to find what is causing his personal or family problems, and to see what he can do to solve them.

Caseworkers are trained for this service of discovering the broad range of human ills and of helping each individual to decide what remedies among those available would be best for him.

Healthy people have pains and worries, and they get over them. So do healthy families. A child gets measles and then gets well. Couples have spats and then make up. Daughters use lipstick too soon, and sons beg for the family car and keep it out too late. We solve these problems and grow on them. Sometimes we can stand even the massive pain of a crippling accident, of war, and unemployment, and still not break.

But sometimes these pressures can overwhelm us. Homes can become so tense that the strain throws out trouble warnings. A child sleeps in school, or he ducks out the door as his father comes up the front steps. Nagging turns to shrill quarrelling. Parents fight over taking in grandparents.

Troubled people worry. They don't know what to do. They lie awake going over their problems while the wires that link up the family pull taut and seem ready to snap.

This is where a caseworker can help. No one should go into casework unless she likes people and enjoys helping them with their way out of trouble towards a happier life. To get her job she has had to go through college and then takes special training, usually in a school of social science. She studies psychology, the family, and society.

Such a school, and the agencies that hire caseworkers, expect her to be intelligent, unprejudiced, and well balanced, and to have good judgment, common sense, and understanding.

She learns how to deal sympathetically with the upset, unhappy ones who will come to her for help. She learns how to look below the surface for the root of the trouble. She learns what tools are to hand to treat the wide array of problems she must meet. There are eye problems, and there are sight-saving classes in schools. Chronic illness can be met with nursing. For aged relatives needing special care there may be rest-homes. She learns to spot problems and to know community resources and to pick the satisfactory clinic or social agency which can best serve each individual case.

Also she works with the personalities in the upset home. Her job is first to understand what is troubling the individual. Then she helps the vexed person himself to understand his problem.

She helps him find inside himself, inside the home, or in health and welfare agencies, the resources to rebuild his family's life. With her help, he chooses those changes he can make in his actions, in his home situation, or his work, that promise to make him and his family happier.

A man may try to dominate his children and find they are getting into one bad scrape after another. He may come to decide he must change his way with them. In himself, with help, he may find enough love for these youngsters to outweigh his pride and his old habits of shouting them into obedience. In even hopeless, beaten people are such stores of love, tolerance, or ability to sacrifice—as when parents must agree to place a child in a foster home to help solve the child's problem and theirs.

Caseworkers set out these discovered inner resources before their clients just as they put before them outside resources like psychiatrists, legal help, or nurseries, or camping chances. They inspire them with confidence enough to face their home realities and to go back willing to change them. That builds the independence needed to take the inset of new daily problems, to solve them by sharing loads and rewards in a home pleasant with mutual respect.

All this is done in friendliness. It is never forced upon people. The client is assured his confidences are safe with someone who wants to help, both for the job of solving a problem and because a good solution will add to the community's order and richness. Casework's help aims to bring the trouble down so that families can take up again that healthy home life which is the small image of our nation's democratic way, and a main source of its strength.

There has been a similar lack of knowledge about caseworkers in Britain until the sixties and this may be partly because here the workers are only now beginning to be trained to use psychological theories and a casework method based on them, which has made the skill of the worker so effective in North America. A small preliminary study published in 1962[1] showed not only a serious lack of knowledge about social work and caseworkers among the public, but, in relation to particular social problems—marital conflicts, for

[1] Noel Timms, "The Public and the Social Worker", *Social Work*, January, 1962, and "Knowledge, Opinion and the Social Services—A Pilot Study", *Sociological Review*, November, 1961.

example—either a serious pessimism in the face of possible help or else a feeling that one ought not to interfere. In the middle of a national economic crisis in 1965 a leading article in a popular sociological journal on how to use the welfare budget[1] largely ignored the positive contribution to general well-being and adequate functioning which can be made by caseworkers, and in a discussion of the major social services, mentioned them only in regard to community care of the mentally ill. The colossal waste involved in having social services administered and staffed largely by untrained people seems to have been unappreciated. We are, however, beginning to experience a change not unlike the growth experience in North America. In the sixties the impact of our welfare legislation has produced no millennium. Welfare provides the structure, within which there is still need for further understanding, compassion, and service to individuals in distress. So the demand has grown for caseworkers with training who could operate within a welfare structure on a basis of individual personal help. As more people trained, the social caseworkers who were practising and teaching began to write books about their practice so that knowledge about casework began to be more generally disseminated among the public.[2] Perhaps the first spotlight was turned on the work through the aggressive attack made on casework by Barbara Wootton in her book *Social Casework and Social Pathology*, published in 1959, and later through the more positive approach of Paul Halmos in *The Faith of the Counsellors*, both of which engaged the interest of people outside social work. The B.B.C. during the autumn and winter of 1965 transmitted an educational television series under the general title of

---

[1] Unsigned article "Making Best Use of the Welfare Budget", *New Society*, 5th August, 1965.

[2] Some typical explanatory literature is: *Introduction to a Social Worker*, National Institute for Social Work Training, George Allen and Unwin, 1964; *Social Work and Social Change*, Dame Eileen Younghusband, George Allen and Unwin, 1964; *The Social Workers*, B.B.C. Publications.

*The Social Workers,* which gave the public an introductory survey of social work, and published a book of essays on social work and welfare intended for people interested in following up the scope of the television broadcasts.

The growing interest in general social work and the use of caseworkers is now being much more valued at Government level and, after the publication of a White Paper[1] at the end of 1965, concerned with the prevention of delinquency, a small independent committee was set up under the chairmanship of Mr Frederick Seebohm to examine the structure of the various services connected with the support of the family and consider their reorganization as a united service. Such a service would lead to a better and more economic deployment of trained social workers, who are not at the moment being trained in anything like sufficient numbers to man all the statutory social services, let alone the voluntary organizations. The mass media of communication, the consciousness of all that is happening in the world, is bombarding people with the personal agonies of mankind, at once sensitizing us, and sometimes also hardening us as a defence against feeling the pain. The close-up communication of television, photography, the spoken broadcast word—all these open up for us distress of a very individualized kind. The question arises as to whether we shall respond knowledgeably, and so compassionately, to the agony of others, or accept it as too big to cope with. One or the other must be done. Action depends on whether we can bear to face up to the pain of human need. The social worker has to face it; can the priest make his theology relevant to it, so that more people can bear to face it? In doing this the priest gives meaning to life and shows the people the way through and the road ahead.

There is a great deal in our society which points to the need for greater sensitivity to human suffering and mental anguish, so that we can do something about it. Suicide, for

[1] *The Child, The Family, and the Young Offender.*

example, is recognized universally as the most flagrant statement of unhappiness which a human being can make. In a recent study Professor Stengel reminds us that approximately 5,500 people have died annually in Great Britain through suicide, a rate of ten to eleven per 100,000 deaths of the general population; and six to eight times that number each year are known to make suicidal attempts from which they recover. These figures are not negligible and, indeed, the statistics of attempted suicide are likely to be an underestimate.[1]

Figures published by the Home Office show that each year a steady figure of five children out of every thousand under the age of eighteen are in the care of the local authority because their own families cannot look after them. A former president of the Children's Officers' Association has estimated that the figure of actual or potentially neglected children who require help in their own homes is about 41 out of every 1,000 children under eighteen.

These figures seem to reflect the difficulties, perhaps one could even call it failure, experienced by a highly industrialized society in functioning as a neighbourhood community and the lack of understanding within it of human emotional conflict.

An examination of the circumstances surrounding both suicide and deprivation reveals a fairly constant aetiology of social isolation and breakdown in personal relationships; similar backgrounds are constant in studies of the more serious problems of the elderly.

It must always be that casework will have a special concern and relevance for underprivileged groups because the nature of an underprivileged environment is always of very great importance in the genesis of a problem, but enough has been said to show that casework help may be needed by anybody at any time, and does not have to be confined to any one group of people. Emotional problems are the nature of life,

[1] Ernst Stengel, *Suicide and Attempted Suicide*, Pelican, 1964.

they cannot be legislated away. What is grossly needed in society to-day is twofold: firstly, a better understanding of the genesis of emotional problems, and secondly an ability to see them in the total context of living. These are the respective fields of the social worker and the priest. In making theology relevant to human need and experience the priest gives understanding of the nature of God, and therefore of the purpose and meaning of life. There is not very much possibility of anyone helping a person with his problem if that person sees no meaning or purpose to his life.

Now facing up to other people's pain and distress also means allowing ourselves to feel into it, to share in it a little, even to be at one with it. This means facing feelings of fear, rejection, pride, and hatred, which lie deep in all of us and which we spend a great deal of psychic energy in dealing with unconsciously, so that we change them into some reaction which wins our self-approval and enables us to feel we have overcome them. To undo all the unconscious psychological work we have done, to uncover what we have been at pains to cover up, can be unbearable. It is not always advisable to ask people to do it. Yet here is a dilemma in society. If society is to help with complex emotional problems, it must first be able to face them. It is precisely because it does not that the social worker is left working largely alone, and looking for support mainly to the psycho-analytical psychiatrist.

This is where the good priest can and does help. Revelation does not deny the analytical explanation of the way man feels and behaves. Indeed the one confirms the other. Christ asks us to face our inmost selves, and the priest must help all of us to do so and in helping us must give us hope and faith about the purpose of life. Thus what our welfare state is doing is requiring the Church to emphasize man in his strength, his ability to face himself and his weakness and to change and grow. It is significant that the strength can come only through weakness, when he asks the question, "Is what I am all right?" Perhaps this is what the cry of dereliction on the Cross was telling us. Only after the Passion is there the Resurrection. So rebirth comes only after facing our inmost selves. The Gospel requires us to care for man, and caring means understanding, but before we begin to understand we must first look at and try to understand ourselves and the purpose in our living. So building up the community of the Church as a caring responsive body means first helping people to face themselves and grow, so that out of this understanding they may be better able to show care for others who need it. So the priest's work is really more basic and primary than the work of the social worker. It comes first, for the reconciling, caring community is needed by everyone.

# 3

## What the Social Worker does

Social caseworkers do not have to have a denominational religious background to do their work effectively. Their skill is a discipline in itself, which we shall look at now. First of all it is based on certain ethical and rational assumptions:

(*a*) that the individual has worth in himself;

(*b*) that it is possible to develop what is worth while in every individual because he has a potential for development—that is, growth, like that of the well-nurtured plant, and not a change which is out of character;

(*c*) that every individual has a right to find his own solution to his problem; a solution which is satisfying to himself and to the society in which he lives;

(*d*) that the community has a responsibility towards the individual in helping him to live in society; this is expressed by the existence of the public social services.

The function of the social caseworker is to solve the problem of his client; usually there is a psychological element in it, always it has social components. He does this by helping the client himself to cope. But the first thing, of course, must be to find out the nature of the problem, which is usually presented in layers—the immediate problem which the client presents, other problems connected with this, and underlying all these a much tougher problem which may be very difficult for the client even to face. For example, let us suppose a man has been referred to a hospital out-patient department, where a diagnosis of duodenal ulcer has been made.

The surgeon tells the man he must have an operation. The man says that he cannot go into hospital, he cannot take time off work, there are important jobs to be completed. The surgeon considers the operation vital and therefore refers him to the medical social worker to see if she can help solve the problem the man presented. As she talks to the man the medical social worker finds that he is worried about various financial commitments he has taken on at home; he has heavy payments on a mortgage, some bills are due shortly for the repair of his old car and for a new garage he has had to put up since the old one he rented was pulled down, he has promised his boy a holiday abroad with the family of a school friend which will be expensive. If he goes into hospital he will lose the overtime rates on which he has been depending, and his obvious exposure of his poor health will jeopardise his chance of promotion, since younger men are in the running. All these are the accompanying problems. The medical social worker has enough knowledge of community resources to know how to help him deal with these: loans can be provided from voluntary funds, which she can arrange for him to pay back as best suits him, and in the circumstances some societies can make a grant for the boy's holiday. But, in fact, these things are not the real underlying problem. Again, as she talks with the man, the medical social worker finds that the thought of the operation has stirred up in him very deep fears about himself and the way he is managing his life. He has never felt that he was able to do all he should as a husband and father, not able to provide enough things, to live up to the concept of head of a family on whom other people could depend. Now the operation is exposing all his inadequacies, his family needs his support, and illness prevents him from giving it. His long-hidden, deep-seated fears come to the fore and are overwhelming him. He feels at heart a failure, wretched and depressed.

The man himself will not have been able to put all this clearly into words. The medical social worker may have taken two or more interviews to come to this diagnosis and will have built it up out of many facts and observations. If she is sure about her diagnosis she will then see her way to help. She will not emphasize the man's fear and insecurity which are the underlying problem, but will use her knowledge to find opportunities to build up his strengths and status. She will help him to see the operation, with its statistics of excellent results, as something which will prevent him from being an ailing man and make him a more effective provider for his family, stressing the good things which she knows he has already done for them, helping him to cope by giving him strength and realistic hope, not false reassurance.

I have said that the medical social worker found out certain things *as she talked*, and this emphasizes the two prerequisites which start the process of casework; they are firstly, the interview, and secondly, the worker-client relationship. The interview is the structured conversation which, for the worker, has to have both focus and purpose. In the beginning the purpose is to find the psycho-social diagnosis, and the worker focuses therefore on what is relevant to finding out. The worker needs to know certain facts, and the client must trust the worker before he can tell them. This trust is the basis of the relationship; it comes from the client's feeling accepted by the worker, whatever he is like, knowing the confidence will be respected, seeing that the worker is looking at the problem with him at his level, not pushing him around, and experiencing that here is someone who knows what to do, is not floundering in the situation as he is himself, but is sure and confident about finding the right way out, a way which is tailored to the client's own individuality, and is not a "common-denominator" piece of advice.

The psycho-social diagnosis has therefore to be a systematized procedure in which the worker brings to bear a specific compendium of knowledge. This knowledge is based on an understanding of human behaviour and the effects on it of stress, an awareness of environmental conditions and personality conflicts and their interaction in the genesis of a problem. Out of this diagnosis there comes an informed understanding which enables the worker to say both "How has this problem come about?" and "What help can I offer to the client which this specific client can use?" The help is not helping the person to adjust, but helping him to cope with his problem, which makes the whole process an individualized one. The worker therefore needs to know the nature of the problem thoroughly, and the process of finding it out —diagnosing—is based on a method of work which is part of the caseworker's skill. What is this method and how has the caseworker come to it?

Caseworkers are heirs to four streams of tradition: first, that of active philanthropy, compassionately concerned about the inarticulate minorities; secondly, that of men's democratic struggle for the right to self-assertion, self-fulfilment, and self-responsibility; thirdly, the assertion of the feeling-part of man, first overtly stressed by the romantic writers and painters at the beginning, significantly, of the machine-age, and later underlined by the theory and practice of Freud and of the analysts; and, fourthly, the inductive thinking of the social scientists. The social casework method is based on principles of accepting the client as he is, evaluating the behaviour but not judging the person; working with him, not behind his back, sharing and discussing together the plans it seems best to make and doing this in an atmosphere of trust which comes from the client's knowing that his confidences will not be betrayed. Its method, like that of the earliest social scientists, is inductive, not purely scientific, because in dealing with the many factors involved we do not have enough knowledge of the kind which can be falsified; but it is an inductive method based on systematized observation. In doing casework, then, there are five steps. One gathers *facts*, in order to determine the nature of the problem. One reassembles the facts, looking for patterns and meaning which they seem to present. One then formulates tentatively a psycho-social diagnosis. Next, and arising out of this diagnosis, comes the casework plan, which is tailored to the individual client and discussed with him. Finally, the caseworker helps the client to put the plan into action and provides the motivation for the client to work on it.

There are two kinds of facts to be gathered—social facts and feeling facts. For example, the statement that Peter is thirteen and has no mother, but has a father and stepmother, are social facts which tell us something about Peter, but not everything. The worker must not jump to conclusions about any of them, thinking that Peter may have a bad stepmother or be a deprived child. More facts will be needed before conclusions can be reached. Some of these will be social—what age was Peter when he lost his mother, what were the circumstances? But some will be related solely to feeling. How does Peter *feel* now about having no mother and having a stepmother? Feelings are of paramount importance. The stepmother may be a good one doing all she can for Peter, but Peter may grudge the fact that she is not his real mother, whose loss he may never have had a chance to mourn properly. So feeling-facts may often distort the social facts and change the surface nature of the problem. This distortion has its antecedent; something happened to make Peter feel this way. All behaviour has meaning, and it is the caseworker's job to find out the meaning. Only then does he begin to see what the problem is about; he does not stop at the surface picture.

So the re-assembling of the facts—both social and feeling-facts—is the part of the caseworker's method which needs the most attention. It is also the most skilled part of the job, where the worker draws on his background of psychology, knowledge of developmental stages in life and the amount of strength or stress they induce, emotional conflicts and the unconscious forces at work in us, cultural factors influencing our social rôles and helping or hindering our coping abilities. As the worker listens and interjects here and there to elicit more facts—When did it all start to get difficult? How did you feel about that? What worries you most about this? —he begins to see the meaning and patterns behind the problem and to make a tentative psycho-social diagnosis. This diagnosis is not a label, it is really a summing-up of the re-assembling, a restatement of the problem including the forces at work within it, personal, familial, social and cultural, economic and psychological. It is out of this summing-up, this restatement, that a plan of help, tailored to this particular client, can be made, and here the worker has to make a choice about what to focus on first. The problem has, as it were, to be broken up into little bits in order to make a start on it. Starting on it then involves some response in the client, and this gives the worker an indication of the rightness or wrongness of his diagnosis. The client's response may bring forward new facts which may cause the worker to revise or confirm his diagnosis of the problem. In working on it with the client, the worker brings to bear the skilled knowledge which he has, and which the client does not have. This, among other things, involves knowledge about the resources in the community which can be used to help.

Let us see from an example how the worker's method could be used in practice. The following is a statement about a thirteen-year-old boy. It reveals that there is a problem. How would the social caseworker view this statement?

PETER, aged 13.

*Home Circumstances.* Peter has no mother, but lives with his father and stepmother. The stepmother has a child of her own, a girl of about five. This girl is a pretty, attractive, intelligent little girl. Both Peter's father and stepmother say that they are rather tired of his behaviour. They seem to be rather disappointed at his lack of progress at school.

*Physical development.* Peter is growing so rapidly that he appears to be much older than his actual chronological age. He is gawky, clumsy, and untidy. He has no specific physical defects. He is left-handed.

*Abilities.* He seems to have a mental age of a child of about 10. He is the dullest and most backward boy in the class. He cannot read and does not seem to be able to do even the simplest sums. He goes to a country school where there is only one class of 20 children between the ages of 11–15, and Peter is the most inefficient of them in class work.

*Behaviour.* He has developed a very aggressive attitude which frequently leads to friction in school and outside, and, of course, also with his father who sometimes gives him "the belt". He bullies younger children and often has fights, particularly during games. In school, if his arithmetic is marked wrong after he has worked a sum, he will either tear up the page or copy the right answer from another child and then mark it right himself. In class he is always eager to put up his hand when a question is asked, but when called upon to give an answer, he is unable to find words to express himself; when someone else gives the right answer, he always says, "That was what I meant to say". This often causes laughter in class, much to Peter's embarrassment.

Of course, no worker would dream of proceeding on these facts alone. The worker approaches the statement knowing that the behaviour has some meaning behind it. The boy is trying to say by his behaviour what he cannot put into words. The worker, therefore, wants more facts. The facts that are there lead the worker to ask for more; the family circumstances and the feelings and rivalries, the nature of the feelings towards Peter, the school situation and teacher's understanding. The facts we have show us only a broad general draft from which to work, but it seems as if Peter is unhappy and probably very angry underneath because his need for unconditional love is not being met. From time to time his anger cannot be contained, and he has outbursts of aggression; he also makes bids for affection and to be approved; these bids do not come off in the way he hopes, but really bring further trouble on him. The worker will want to work on the problem, therefore, of Peter's unhappiness, working with Peter and his parents primarily, and possibly, if the parents wish, helping the school to understand Peter's problem. The worker will have to be prepared for a lot of aggression in Peter, and to take on himself, without getting angry or hurt, the hostility which Peter really feels for other people. The worker may want to find for Peter some more socially acceptable form of expressing his aggression, in wrestling or climbing or boxing, and will try to provide some gratification for him—he needs not only to be protected from pain but also helped to find pleasure. At some stage the worker might ask Peter what he would like life to be if it could be as he wanted. This would help the worker to understand Peter's needs and deprivations and so begin to plan towards correcting them. He would then also see more clearly the kind of gratification Peter needed, and also how far he was living in a fantasy world and how much the worker would have to help him face reality. The worker's knowledge of the psychology of adolescence will be important here. The worker's job with the parents will be supportive and interpretative. They might be asked why they think Peter is behaving like this and helped to see some of the problems he has had in growing up. The real focus of help will be on the interaction between Peter and his parents. A child builds up opinions and attitudes about himself by the way his parents react to him in times of stress. Here a vicious circle has been set up and the worker will have to change this into a benign one.

It will be seen that in this way of working the worker has at no time put pressure on Peter either to conform to different standards or to accept coaching for lessons. The emotional tension under which Peter is labouring may very well be responsible for his backwardness and he will not respond to learning pressures till the tension is relieved. The worker is going to concentrate on lessening the emotional tension (the underlying problem) and, if he succeeds, the learning problem (accompanying problem), and the behaviour problem (presenting problem) will reduce themselves. The worker does not work by means of pressure, but on a very different basis which involves an understanding of personality and the defences used by the personality to relieve and master tension, which is crucial to the whole casework process. This understanding of personality can best be described diagrammatically.

Man is in continual conflict between two forces—I want and I ought. The "doing", behaviour part of us is really a test of whether we have found a balance between these two pressures.

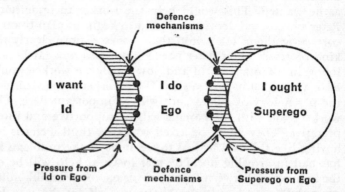

The doing, executive part of us, is the part the outside world sees, the decisive part of the self, reconciling our internal needs with the reality of the external world. In psychological terms it is called the ego. In its decision-making it uses many things—memory, cognition, evaluation, and defences against pain. The wanting part of us is really a reservoir of instinctive impulses which are pleasurable, they derive from our physiology and are an important part of our humanity. The pressures of the instincts remain throughout our whole lives, though they vary quantitatively at different stages of our development. We call this part of our personality the id. It is full of tremendous energy, which is instinctual, and this powerful energy, which is always seeking discharge, is known as libido.

From birth the human personality has the ego-task of reconciling these instinctual pleasures with the reality of the world in which it lives. This means that society exerts some influence on personality. This begins in the earliest days when the mother first starts to handle the child. Gradually, in a few months, he learns to wait more confidently and less agonizedly for his food because he has learned by experience that mother does always bring it; his ego has begun to reconcile his need for food with his need to wait while he sees mother preparing it. This control on his behaviour is the part played in our personality by civilization as opposed to the instincts. It is known as the superego and it forces the ego to deal with the pressures from the id in a more sophisticated way than the id would want. The origin of the superego is the edicts of one's parents, the process of education that the parents or other parental figures give the child by example and teaching. The ego imposes control on the instincts because the child wants to be loved by his parents and so he behaves as they want him to. In the very beginning the child submits to the will of the parents in order to survive, and later because he fears the loss of their love. The process of civilization is therefore really built on love. Children who have been reared on fear of punishment rather than love will throw off the standards at adolescence, and the process of re-education has to start all over again. All adolescents go through the process of evaluating again the standards they have incorporated in childhood. These have to be submitted to the test of their reasoning—a task of the ego. This is why properly thought-out explanations of the rationale of morality are so crucial at this time. The child's superego— "you ought"—is in the process of being thrown off and the ego will accept only a control whose values it respects. This is what man's freedom means. It is still based on love. There is a big task for theologians now to interpret Christian morality and ethics in the light of the contemporary new knowledge available to us from the disciplines of psychology, anthropology, and sociology. The criteria for accepted ethics are rethought out by adolescents in each generation, and this creates the new culture pattern of each ensuing generation, and the new adult internalized superego in each individual.

From this it will be seen that there is no period in life when the ego is not working hard to maintain itself in an equilibrium between the forces of "I want" and "I ought". Sometimes the pressures of one or the other or both become very strong and the ego tends to bend between them. In an effort to avoid breaking, the ego throws up "muscles", as it were, to maintain itself in equilibrium; we can call these muscles the defences. They distort the way the ego acts, and it is this distortion which makes behaviour often seem so difficult to understand. The mechanisms of defence are mechanisms of the ego to allay anxiety and relieve tensions. The ego must use them or break; they are normal, healthy manœuvres and must not be regarded as pathological. The use of defences shows that the ego is under strain and that the individual is struggling to deal with it. Sometimes the defences achieve their purpose; sublimation and identification are two common defences which enable individuals to go on functioning in a socially acceptable way; some defences, like regression, or projection, while they effectively deal with the person's inner anxiety so that he does not experience it as intolerable, will often upset other people so that he acquires a social and personal emotional problem. So a vicious circle has been set up. This is usually the predicament a person is in when the social worker is asked to help.

The worker therefore must be able to recognize the defences, understand their genesis, and look for the underlying cause of pain. It will be seen that it would be fatal for the worker *at this time* to increase the pressure exerted by the superego by something as crude as saying, "Try to pull yourself together" or using moral exhortation. This only increases the pressure exerted by the superego and produces fear of loss of love, which is really what we mean by guilt. This in turn explains why guilt is so paralysing and why it needs to be "washed away" by acts which *prove* love (i.e. Christ's death *for us*. . . . "These are they which came out of great tribulation, and have washed their robes and made them white in the blood of the lamb.") The ego is trying to pull itself together by using the defences and cannot do more without help. The worker's task is to give that help, and this means strengthening the ego. How does one do this?

The answer to this question is found by looking at the way the ego "grows". We have seen that this came about by the child's wanting to be loved. The love of the parents strengthened the little child's ego to deal with the task of subduing his instinctual demands to the edicts he was being taught. Most of our conflicts in later life stem from the earlier struggles we had at crucial periods of our development when we were trying to do this. The struggles left residuals which are reactivated at all periods of crisis in later life. These crises are therefore important experiences when our earlier failures or successes can be reinforced or corrected. These crisis situations are also the areas usually most open to the ministrations of the priest.

The worker's support of the ego is given by the method of his work. Crucial to this method is the worker/client relationship. The relationship is built on acceptance of the client as a person of value *as he is*, on confidentiality, on participation in planning together, on the hope that the worker gives the client through the mastery he shows of his job, on his competence as he works towards a diagnosis, and on his showing to the client that there is a way to help. This is realist hope, not false reassurances which would be a betrayal of the client's trust. This sort of love and hope is technical and specific, controlled and analysed, as it were, in relation to a particular task. It is the *specificity* of it and not the general nature of it which helps the client in his situation. But now it will also be seen how supportive are these general qualities of love and realist hope in the community which are strengthening all our approaches to the tasks of life. We see again the need for interpretation in contemporary terms of the nurturing experience of the Gospel of love and hope, for which the priest is needed as an expert. Casework is concerned with helping people to cope with a specific problem. The priest is concerned with man's coping with the whole of life, and understanding its meaning and purpose. Nevertheless, he needs to know also how to recognize when a problem is there and, more important, how to recognize whether his parishioner wants to be helped. Looking systematically at the facts will help him to assess whether there is a problem; to assess whether his parishioner needs help he will have to "listen" to what the behaviour is really trying to say. This means understanding behaviour, not just in rational terms. but in terms of stress and defence.

# 4

## *Experience and Stress*

Let us look at the relevance to the priest of what we have been saying. We have looked at what the social worker does. But the priest has always been concerned with pastoral care, a watching, guarding, comforting, guiding based on compassion and disciplined self-awareness. The compassion and self-awareness are the common bond between the priest and the caseworker; the differences lie in the different ends of the two workers. The social worker aims with the client to reach certain goals which will mean the solving of his specific problem. Usually the aim of the priest is much bigger than this, and provides the groundwork and strength for the whole business of living. In the course of his bigger job, the priest can help with the solving of a specific problem, too, and can work with the caseworker in a number of ways. First, he gives hope and purpose and meaning to life; secondly, his understanding of behaviour helps him to accept rather than judge, and this supports a person to have faith in himself and to work with the social worker towards what may be a very difficult goal for him. The Church's administration also provides opportunity for the priest to be there at times of crisis or potentiality in all people's lives—marriage, births of children, education, adolescence, death, and bereavement. At these times the pastoral rôle of the parish priest is to give guidance, understanding, comfort, and care. In doing so continually he can often by his support prevent the building up of stresses into problems which can sometimes become so cumulative that specialist social work is needed to sort them out and solve them. To do his job the priest really needs to know a lot about the mechanics of behaviour as well as what is meant by the relationship of God to man, man's purpose and God's acceptance. Emotional situations are the stuff of life, they make for personality growth, but they are also crises which carry potential danger. This means that the individual experiencing them needs understanding and acceptance at the time. The stress may bring forth defensive behaviour which is misunderstood, and the resultant criticism increases the damage and feelings of inadequacy. Quite severe changes in behaviour may be seen at these times, and the priest who is ministering needs to understand them in order that his own feelings of despair or irritation at what may seem unreasonable conduct may be changed or controlled. People who do not understand the mechanisms of defence tend to lash back or withdraw with feelings of anger or hurt at their manifestation. The person who understands that the defence indicates pain is supportive to the client, and support helps the client to cope better himself with what is happening, because it is an assurance of love and concern, which is the climate in which personality growth takes place.

Stress, then, has to be seen as a disturbance of the ego's equilibrium which causes the defences to be brought into play in order to try to cope. But when the individual can deal with the stress, this is an enlarging, nourishing experience for the ego, and in this way stress can be seen as carrying the potential for ego development. Stress deforms when it engenders defences which by their nature bring the individual into further difficulty, as in the case of Peter in Chapter 3, or when it is so great that even the useful defences are broken down. Stresses therefore do not have an intrinsic quality by which they are measurable. They should be looked at from the point of view of what they mean to the individual, and what they do to those in close relationship to the individual. This means an individual specific assessment in each case, and not a general common-denominator judgement. What makes a situation stressful to one person and not to another is determined by the cumulative effect of the individual's previous life experiences, his temperament, feelings, and constitution, the age at which he is required to bear the stress, and the cultural factors which aid or impede him in bearing it. There is usually some "last straw" which is the precipitating factor in making the stress unbearable, but this last straw can usually be seen as the *occasion* for the crisis and not the cause. The concept of multiple causation is crucial to the social worker's understanding of problems and diagnosis.

Stresses fall into two groups: those with which we are all familiar and which we must expect to go through, and those which are unusual. There is less understanding in the community about the unusual stresses, and therefore less support given to the people who endure them.

The first, usual sort of stresses we all experience; they are those connected with physiological growth, which occur at vulnerable ages. There is the very great stress of the infant in the first month of life, who has to learn to cope with the change from the oneness with the mother's living body to separation from it—to change the dark, warm enclosed womb for the bright light, changing temperature, and noise of living, experiencing now hunger and learning to wait for food. It is not for nothing that this first month of life is regarded in public health as the most vulnerable stage of a child's existence. Adolescence is another familiar time of stress; biological needs increase the pressure on the ego, while the parental commands absorbed in childhood tend to be thrown off—indeed, social approval of heterosexual interests means that traits encouraged in childhood *must* be cast off if the person is ever to become adult. So the ego, pressed by the id and robbed of the balance of the superego, loses its equilibrium. This is the explanation of most adolescent conflict, and its manifestation in changeable moods and defences has a psychological as well as a physiological basis. The integration of an adult superego is now a major task of adolescence. Similar disturbance of equilibrium occurs round about the menopause in women and the climacteric in men. Pressures from the id fluctuate, intensifying and waning in response to physiological changes, and the importance of a properly integrated superego, which gives balance, can lessen some of the stress, but some of the uncharacteristic behaviour which occurs at this time is the ego's defensive response to the pressure and strain. Both these periods, however, also serve as a means to ego development as the individual learns to cope, and he goes forward into the next stage of life with added psychic strength and maturity. The final physiological stress phase is in old age, when weakened energy threatens the integrity of the ego. The ego tries desperately to go on functioning in accustomed ways so that the person becomes like an overdrawn portrait. We say as folk grow old that they are like themselves, only more so. This "more-so-ness" has to be seen as the attempt of the personality to hold itself together. What defences have existed will be intensified; it is the ego's final manœuvring to preserve itself intact. The fear with which old age is regarded in the community—in contrast to the attraction of childhood—robs the ego of any nurturing support of assurance of love and concern. Here a quotation from Peter Townsend's study published in 1962,[1] of the living conditions of the elderly is not inappropriate. The author says that the origins of his research actually lay "in a single visit paid a few years ago to a large institution which had been a workhouse. I was not prepared for what I saw and a brief account of my observations may help to explain why research appeared to be justified."

A high wall surrounded some tall Victorian buildings, and the entrance lay under a forbidding arch with a porter's lodge at one side ... there was no garden worthy of the name. Several hundred residents were housed in large rooms on three floors. Dormitories were overcrowded, with ten or twenty iron-framed beds close together, no floor covering and little furniture other than ramshackle lockers. The day rooms were bleak and un-

[1] *The Last Refuge*, Peter Townsend, Routledge and Kegan Paul, London, pp. 4, 5.

inviting. In one of them sat forty men in high-backed Windsor chairs, staring straight ahead or down at the floor. They seemed oblivious of what was going on around them. The sun was shining outside, but no-one was looking that way. Some were seated in readiness at the bare tables even though the midday meal was not to be served for over an hour. Watery-eyed and feeble, they looked suspiciously at our troupe of observers and then returned to their self-imposed contemplation. Life seemed to have been drained out from them, all but the dregs. Their stoic resignation seemed attributable not only to infirmity and old age. They were like people who had taken so much punishment that they had become inured to pain and robbed of all initiative. They had the air of not worrying much about their problems because of the impossibility of sorting them out, or the difficulty of getting anyone to understand or take notice. ...

As I walked round the building and discussed the daily routines it seemed that the staff took the attitude that the old people had surrendered any claims to privacy. The residents were washed and dressed and conveniently arranged in chairs and beds—almost as if they were made ready for daily inspection. An attendant was always present in the bathroom, irrespective of the old people's capacity to bath themselves. The lavatories could not be locked and there were large spaces at the top and bottom of the doors. The matron swung one door and unfortunately revealed a blind old woman installed on the w.c. She made no apology.

Some of the features here are obviously a result of trying to administer a home where illness and fragility are ever-present, but concrete evidence of concern does not really seem to be built into the system in any positive way.

Somehow the fear and hatred of old age in the community which this particular home so vividly expressed has got to be turned into acceptance and hope. Here is a paradigm. Can the priest give a positive meaning to age in the light of the gospel which will help men to accept it and the community to make it a time of meaning for them? Canon Peter Green[1] held that it is the time allowed us for coming to terms with what we have made of life, and so a chance to come to our end in peace and hope. Here the priest has great opportunities in his pastoral care and can listen to and use the

[1] *Old Age and the Life to Come*, Mowbray, 1950.

reminiscences of the elderly in a way spiritually healing for them.

Other usual stresses are failures, frustrations, bereavements, and lastly, environmental conditions which we cannot ourselves control. Stress also occurs when our accustomed rôle in life is threatened. This may affect our relationships or our status, and sometimes both. Family rôles dissolve, and there has to be a realignment; when a father dies a widowed mother has to take on a different rôle with added tasks to which she is not accustomed, or an adolescent son has to take on heavy responsibilities. When one member of a family leaves home or becomes seriously ill, the familiar rôles of all the other members are threatened and often changed, and the personality is under strain while learning to adjust and cope. Similarly there is a new rôle alignment in the periods just before and after marriage, at the birth of the first child, again at the birth of subsequent children, at a removal from a familiar place to one unknown, at change of school or job.

Unusual stresses occur in various ways—serious illness, operation, a child loses his mother or father, parents have a mentally deficient child, a wealthy man loses all his money, accidents cause permanent injury and incapacity. In each case the individual will have to develop some defence to deal with the stress which will become ingrained in the personality, unless support is forthcoming to help him to bear and cope with it.

Now it will be seen that many of the situations we have mentioned are those with which the priest is concerned: young children are brought soon after birth to be baptized, some Churches have schools and therefore there can be contact with families who come new to the district; marriage, sickness, bereavement, churching, are his pastoral ministry. It is important that he does not ignore the psychology implicit in the situation and the quantitatively different stress potential in all of them. These stress situations *can* affect our capacity to cope, to deal with our inner needs and reconcile them with the reality of living; in psychological terms they impair our ego functioning and cause us inevitably to throw up defences to deal with them. These defences safeguard the personality against disintegration, and we must not therefore attack them. To do so would leave the vulnerable ego exposed and it could then (and does) break down. We must therefore be able to recognize some of the major defences, and while recognizing them remember their positive function for the ego's task of coping with life. We need to look at them in relation to the individual's age, state of maturation, individual development, and also in relation to the pressure of the situation, whether they are appropriate to the amount of stress, whether they respond to help; that is, whether the defences are used in all sorts of situations or only in some situations. This then gives us understanding of what the real areas of conflict are.

Most people will recognize in themselves, as well as in others, the defences used by the ego. Three common defences are helpful to the ego in its attempts to deal with the business of living—compensation, sublimation, and identification. Lost or unobtainable things can be compensated for: the boy with a residual limp following poliomyelitis spends all his time with his motor bike which gives him speed and mobility; Josephine Butler, after the death of her child, turned to helping unmarried mothers; she went out, in her own words, "to seek a sorrow greater than my own"; achievement or possessions may be substituted for love relationships, and so on. In sublimation early unacceptable instincts may be channelled into socially acceptable forms; aggression channelled into sport is an obvious example. But early intra-psychic conflict is often channelled into creative or academic work, into collecting treasures or into revolt from or interpretation of authority. We also identify with those whom we admire, with causes which express our inner fears or hopes, and so some of our pain and anxiety can be dealt with effectively in this unconscious way, through identifying with something successfully achieved.

Fragmentary and temporary regressions are also common defences; the individual shows behaviour which is immature for his stage of development. Usually this is an unconscious flight to an earlier life period when he felt more comfortable and safe, or when he experienced severe conflict, which may have become reactivated. So the individual appears for a time to be behaving inappropriately and immaturely. Regression, however, often operates adaptively; it is like the manœuvre of an army which retreats to re-equip and to put its forces in order and then go into attack. It can therefore be a means to growth and change if the defence is not broken down prematurely. The person who has regressed needs concrete help with the problem, not the breaking-down of his defence, just as the army in retreat needs reinforcements.

Repression is the process whereby something which could be conscious is held down in unconsciousness—so there can be blocking, some forgetting or amnesia about a painful period of life. In reaction formation the defence operates so that the ego does the opposite of what the impulse prompts him to do, so that we are kind when we really hate, because hate is not acceptable to us and therefore painful to us, or we hate where we really love because in this way we cover up our expected rejection by the loved person. In undoing, the person, once he has started on some action, starts unconsciously to undo the effects of it. Lady Macbeth washed out her murder in a sleepwalker's dream. In isolation the feeling which is appropriate to the impulse is defended against by isolating it from the idea, and the person talks with no feeling or expression about his anguish. In projection the ego refuses to allow the personality to recognize something unacceptable to consciousness and so projects it on to someone else, usually using some basis in reality, so we get the "lily-white-hen", recognized in old country speech, the person who is never to blame for his own faults. Introjection is when the ego turns upon itself feelings which it would really prefer not to have, so hatred or aggression felt towards another person or a community may be turned upon oneself, producing depression, or, in extreme cases, suicide. In provocation the person provokes someone else to do what he wants but cannot do himself, so although he cannot be hostile to his employer, he can provoke his employer to be hostile to him, dismiss him, and so give him a realist, rational excuse for expressing his hostility openly.

These contortions of the personality are unconscious mechanisms of the individual's defence. Because of something in the history of the person—at some point in his life there has been pain and anxiety about the gratification of some impulse about feeling and emotion—the ego has learned to deal with the experience so that its pain is diminished. Therefore, it will now be clear that some of our behaviour is unconscious, and, particularly when we are upset, it is not wholly rational or even based on the reality of the situation. We carry into emotional situations the residuals of earlier experiences and conflicts which we have not resolved. An example of this is the case of Mr Jerome:

Mr Jerome is aged 54, a widower, employed at night on maintenance work in a generating station. He has three children, two boys aged 18 and 15, and a girl aged 12, at school. The fifteen-year-old boy, Frank, is backward and Mr Jerome worries because he does not seem to make the progress he should. Although the school medical officer was satisfied with the boy's progress, Mr Jerome asked for a hospital consultation for Frank. Frank was seen, but the consultant found him perfectly fit physically, though mentally retarded. The medical social worker was asked to see Mr Jerome.

Mr Jerome presented himself, a tired, rather confused man, easily moved to tears when discussing his wife's sudden death from thrombosis a year before. He found it difficult to put into words what he had to say and could not elaborate or illustrate. He had run the house and looked after the children himself over the last year, without any help. As a result he had very little sleep. Responsibility for Frank lay heavily on him; he saw the boy as dependent on him and he worried about his future and what would happen to him when he himself died. He did not think the teachers gave enough thought to Frank, or took enough trouble over him. He thought a psychiatrist could make Frank different.

Here the social facts and feeling-facts show us an unhappy man, trying by overwork to stop himself from thinking too much, and worrying about his capacity to look after Frank since his mother died. He was hoping at heart that the teachers would take on a more parental rôle and that the psychiatrist would perform a miracle. These phantasies helped him to cope with his inner pain but kept him out of touch with the reality of the situation.

With Mr Jerome's permission the medical social worker got in touch with the school authorities and found that Frank was in a school for educationally subnormal children. He had no special problems there, was likeable and happy, and had not presented any difficulties himself. To the medical social worker it seemed that Mr Jerome might be exaggerating Frank's helplessness and that there was a reason for this. The most likely explanation was that Mr. Jerome had strong feelings about Frank, and he distorted the situation as it was in reality.

The medical social worker, therefore, tried to help Mr Jerome to talk about all the things that bothered him. He talked a lot about his wife's death and seemed greatly helped by putting his feelings into words. The worker also tried to help him plan his day so that he was not so tired. She suggested various social services which might help him and eventually, at his request, made an appointment for him to see a caseworker at the Family Welfare Association, who could help on a long-term basis.

Mr Jerome went to the caseworker at the Family Welfare Association. The caseworker had a longer period to get to know Mr Jerome and therefore discovered more facts which enabled her to work towards a psycho-social diagnosis. Mr Jerome again at first presented his problem around Frank, but he used this to express a tremendous amount of unhappiness over his wife's death and linked this with the death of his own mother which apparently occurred in similar circumstances to the death of his wife. His mother died when he was Frank's age, and he and his brothers and sister continued to maintain a home in his father's household. Mr Jerome described his father's life in his old age as being a lonely and unwanted one, and he was terribly afraid that he would experience this in the years to come.

Now we can begin to understand some of Mr Jerome's unhappiness and confusion. His wife's death, tragic in itself, had reactivated all the early fears and helplessness he experienced when his mother died. These fears distort the reality of the situation for him in the present, and he projects some of it on to Frank. Also his situation now is like that of his own father then, and he is therefore confused about his own identity and afraid that things will work out for him as they did for his father. The caseworker helps him first by helping him to talk out his feelings about his mother's death and come to terms with all he felt about it, which he had kept bottled up. People need time to grieve and mourn, and it is a serious matter that our culture denies this to them. The worker can then give hope to Mr Jerome about the reality of the situation, Frank's success at the school, the relatives who are willing to help, the social services which can support. Through realist hope, concern, and knowledge, the worker offers a solution on which Mr Jerome can work. This could not be done without understanding the theory of mourning and reaction to loss, and the important part played by the release of feelings in helping us to become our truest selves, rather than to remain the prisoner of our own defences. It will take a long time for Mr Jerome to work through his childhood feelings. But the worker's listening, understanding, guiding, and acceptance in the interview will be therapeutic.

This case is not very dissimilar from those presented to the parish priest. He would recognize that a problem existed, first of all by the anxiety which Mr Jerome showed, reflected in his inability to see any strengths in the situation, and later by his exaggeration of his son's problem, his projection of his own anxiety on to the boy, and by his blocking—his inability to do anything to build on the assets in the situation.

He could offer someone like Mr Jerome some concrete help perhaps by talking to Frank's headmaster, whom he personally knows, and by putting Mr Jerome in touch with a helpful neighbour, stressing the good things Mr Jerome and his wife had shared together and emphasizing the positives, underlined by the assurance of a God who is love. Sometimes this is enough support to set people on the road to grappling with life again; sometimes they need longer time to unburden themselves before what the priest says means anything, or even before they can hear it. The powers of absolution, of remembering in prayer, and for guiding wisely a caring and reconciling community, which the priest has, should not be underestimated. If none of this helped Mr Jerome, if he still seemed depressed and concerned about Frank, then the priest might feel that it would be advisable to consult a social worker, perhaps a family caseworker, as to whether anything more specific could be done to help him.

# 5

## Priests and Social Workers

Caseworkers do not have a monopoly of compassion or understanding of human nature. Artists, novelists, poets, and priests are some of the people who have it outstandingly and had it before them. The caseworker's skill is in his ability to understand clearly what the problem is about and the *integration* of three disciplined bodies of knowledge about human behaviour, about methods of help, about community resources to be used, which enables him to plan help with the client. The *disciplined* use of himself in his work, which has to grow through his own self-awareness, he shares with others. The priest, too, has developed this quality of self-awareness; it has been part of the priestly discipline from the beginning of time. So there are these two "bridge areas" as it were of compassion and use of self, where the priest and caseworker meet. Before we can consider how they can work more effectively together, let us look at the reasons why caseworkers have to discipline themselves for their work. First of all, they are working always in the field of problems. Unless there is a problem, caseworkers are not needed. Casework is problem-solving work; there is always some stress, often of a highly emotional nature, often deeply bound to past experiences. Caseworkers in their training have to learn to face their own inner anxieties in order that their defences shall not get the upper hand of them and thereby prevent them from seeing clearly what the emotional situation means *to the client*. The worker's insight into his own defences means that he can be freed from the disabilities of his own past experience and that the client's need is given precedence over his own. This is why the caseworker's relationship is not the same thing as friendship, where there is a mutual acknowledgement of reciprocal need, friend gratifying friend and taking from each other. The gaining of such insight is a slow process, because the phenomenon of resistance operates to prevent us from penetrating to the unconscious layers of our mind and seeing our inmost selves. The whole process of becoming aware is really an emotional one but it is also rather like the process of intellectual growth in a child. Confusion and insight go on together, and then there is a period of consolidation in which understanding and growth comes and then one goes forward to the next growth stage. The psychological insight comes from inside the worker as a result of the knowledge he acquires in the classroom, but also through the clarification of this knowledge as he applies it in his work, and, perhaps above all through the support he is given by his supervisor while in the social agency and his tutor in the training institution. Such insight into *unconscious* mechanisms is to enable the caseworker to use himself fully for others; it is not required, or even encouraged, in the caseworker's clients, but many of them find the support and acceptance they experience from the worker a releasing process and do come to look at their *conscious* selves in a new way, and at the effects of their behaviour in their relationships with other people. They are usually only able to do this after a long period of testing out the worker, so that they are really sure that the worker is a helping person who accepts them with all their faults and mistakes and who still values and believes in them notwithstanding. So the insight into self, at the different levels of client and worker, are both dependent upon experience of acceptance and hope. The worker's acceptance of the client's vulnerability and frailty is in some faint sense a mediation of the unconditional love we all long to experience, and the hope the worker offers that there is a way to help is a mediation of the Christian hope that love is stronger than evil or death.

Within these two experiences the person begins to grow and change. There is a story told by an elderly visitor in a Manchester prison, who remembers a prisoner of good background who came back into gaol six or seven times. On the seventh he told the visitor, "I am the prodigal." He had, he said, got the word from the Bible. The visitor reminded him that the word never appeared in the Bible story. It said, in fact, that a certain man had two sons. "I told him, 'You are a *son*'. He said he would never come back again, and he never did." But the moral of this story is not that he never came back but that if he had come back seventy times seven he would still be a son, and understanding this, through the mediating experience of acceptance by the elderly visitor, was the beginning of the strength in the young man. So, from the depth of his prison experience, Bonhoeffer wrote, "The Christian hope sends a man back to his life on earth in a wholly new way, which is even more sharply defined than it is in the Old Testament." The priest's function is to work with people and their experience and to define the new way, not just in moral terms, but in depths of human and spiritual experience. To make the experience of Christ's way real is the task of the Church. If he is to build communities, the priest must begin individually with the men and women who make them up. The great experiences of life, whether of joy or sadness, at which so often the priest has the task of officiating, leave us changed. There in the situation is defeat and despair or grappling and growth, and it is this situational and psychological area which seems to be the ground for dialogue between the priests and social workers. The priest's interpretation of the Gospel way is crucial to the attitude we bring to the formative crisis-situations in our lives and to the use we make of such crises. The struggle of the ego which we have looked at by an understanding of the defence mechanisms shows human personality turning defeat into something like victory. Out of psychic conflict, producing feelings of failure, inadequacy, and guilt, there come compensation, sublimation, and other defences which absorb the dynamic energy in the id and enable it to be discharged in ways which satisfy and bring contentment. Out of pain and anguish comes a new way of coping, a rebirth, a growth, a resurrection which needs to be nourished by purpose. And this rebirth is like the redemption, and the purpose is the pattern of the Kingdom. In a world of poverty, hunger, and disease it has been pointless to many people to talk about such things. But, when society becomes an enabling experience, then the Gospel has another dimension and Christ of the Resurrection is real. Social workers, in helping people to find new ways of coping, take part as instruments in the work of redemption. But the priest can use the whole of life's experience to reveal God to man in a way which sets him free.

Two of the most fundamental gifts which the priest can bring to people, as part of his special function, are a meaningful understanding of prayer and the symbolism of the sacraments. Prayer brings to happy people, as well as those who are estranged and frightened, a sense of sharing in a great community of human souls who have lived and died united by love and hope and common purpose. It gives a sense of continuity to a person, a sense of being part of the unending cloud of witness of the Church, made up of those who are living, dead, and yet unborn. His life is thus shared and sharing, and in liturgical prayer one is conscious of this lending and borrowing of strength between all sorts of human conditions, so that the sense of eternity and brotherhood can begin to have more meaning, even for very isolated people, and there begins to be an understanding of a transfigured world and a sharing in it. These things help people to live more abundantly.

The sacraments confirm, in a way which rings true to our human nature, the teaching of the Gospel about the nature, condition, and destiny of man. In tangible, material, and visible ways, which sink deeply into the personality's experience, they confirm the doctrines of forgiveness, restoration, unconditional love, and the renewal of life. Like the seals of a contract, they give a reality and permanence to fundamental concepts.

The priest therefore can help us to set the sorrows, joys, sins, and struggles of our life in an eternal framework. It should be the priest who sees the significance of the crisis and problem-solving and helps them to fall into place in the pattern of a person's life, and so truly reorientates the mind, giving hope and purpose. The contribution which the Church can make is therefore a primary one, for it enables people to face calmly their inmost selves with the support of faith and hope, and the sureness of God's acceptance and love.

So before the resurrection must come the cry of dereliction —when Christ shares in man's fear as he asks himself, "Is what I am all right?" The passion teaches us that the strength to face this question comes not only from experience but from having felt God's acceptance, his belief in man. Faced with this astounding affirmation, there is no disaster, no situation, no darkness where the priest cannot bring help of far greater significance and import than the caseworker can approach. All this emphasizes the paramount importance of the priest's work with individuals in making God's acceptance real. He begins there.

Now let us look at the importance of the priest's work with groups and with the larger community. Can he learn anything from the social worker's method of work with groups? What is the social worker trying to do? To the social worker group work is one method of helping individuals. Casework can be used within it, but it has a dimension which is different from casework and is derived from the importance of group experiences in the growth and development of all of us. In our early childhood the group draws the child out from being an egocentric person who recognizes only the presence of others, to becoming someone who recognizes that other people have personalities and independent purposes. The child learns this through the give and take which comes from playing—and fighting—with others in the group; that is, he learns to become a social being through his interaction with others. Here the group leader—the teacher in infant or nursery school—takes over the function of a superego for the child and sets limits to the child's hate, aggression, and fear. This relieves his inner tension, and the comradeship of other children gives him support against the anxieties he feels. In the group experience of the young child he comes in contact with the real world of interacting personalities, and the leader and teacher is helping him to learn to become effective in it while keeping his self-respect, feeling needed, and feeling loved. After being away sick he has been missed by the other children; he is aware that he is liked, not just for what he does, but, unconditionally, for what he is.

From his understanding of group experience the social worker with groups is concerned about the use and development of relationships among members of the group, while the meaning of the group to the members within it is something to be used constructively to involve them in interaction. Interaction and purpose within the group are the two main things the worker must keep clear: what is the purpose of this group, how can it be achieved through the interaction of all the people within it? People are helped to be involved both in the purpose and with each other at the same time. There can be no separation of these two things.

This seems to be a good model of what a parish group should be about, and it is the priest's job to make clear the purpose, the "new way", the revelation towards which we work through involvement with each other, understanding, feeling, learning to be at one, gaining strength both from the purpose and the involvement simultaneously. Here is the leading, teaching function of the priest in the whole field of human living, a function which no-one else shares with him; it is his own specific rôle, laid on him as a commandment by Christ himself.

As he fulfils his teaching function, his showing of the purpose and way revealed in the New Testament, the priest is inevitably aware, as are his parishioners, of the differences between what is set before us there, and the reality. Part of his work is to foster compassion, sensitivity, and action in the Christian laity. The whole Church, therefore—priest, synods, council, and all its members—must be involved in what secular organizations are doing and in statutory responsibility. Out of his understanding of theology the priest can see and proclaim the things that belong to the Kingdom of Heaven on earth; he, as well as the social worker, is involved in community organization. Many priests feel called to do this work actively and to involve social workers appointed and paid by the Church to help. There have been, and are, many experiments; for example, attempting to cope with the failure of state housing policy to meet people's needs, such as the experiment in Hertfordshire in the 1950s[1] and the Sparkbrook Association in a downtown area[2] of Birmingham, which in 1964 founded a Family Centre to provide material and spiritual help in a badly depressed area. In the Gloucester diocese the churches and voluntary organizations have co-operated with the local marriage guidance council and education authority in a scheme for education in personal and family relationships concentrating its resources on the training of teachers and group leaders.[3] The Church's own social workers—historically known as moral welfare workers—have been shown in Miss Hall's and Miss Howe's study to be, by the nature of their work, too isolated from the clergy, whom they might have stimulated by their expert knowledge of community needs. The time has come when the Church has to rethink out its rôle in social action to-day, and to see what sort of more effective impact needs to be made as part of its caring witness, and how it can best influence

[1] Edward le Grice, "The Boreham Wood Experiment" in *Moral Welfare*, April, 1959, and M. Penelope Hall and Ismene V. Howes, *The Church in Social Work*: A Study of Moral Welfare Work undertaken by the Church of England, Routledge and Kegan Paul, 1965, pp. 226–37.

[2] See the article "Pastoral Care and Social Work" by A. H. Denney in *Case Conference*, vol. 12, No. 3, July, 1965.

[3] "Grasping the Nettle", article by Mary Seacome in *Crucible*, November, 1964.

social thinking and social action. Such changes involve dialogues between theologians and social workers, and perhaps different approaches to recruitment and training in the ministry. The social workers themselves need the support and prayers of the Church, and some clear guidance about the rationality of the moral values for which, as social workers, they stand. New patterns of community life are needed, which are examples of care, commitment, and concern within the world.

Perhaps the problem of our time has been the growth of meaningless communities and people who feel "unattached". From this stems much unhappiness—suicide, deprivation, mental illness, delinquency. We still have, within a welfare state, elderly people living in chronic poverty in pitiful conditions, fatherless families lacking emotional as well as financial support, appalling housing, oversized classes, undermanned social services. People cut themselves off from society or openly flaunt and attack it, because it seems so meaningless to them. We need constantly the help of the priest to look at our standards and see whether they have rationality and relevance in the light of both modern knowledge and gospel interpretation; in our moral and religious thinking we need to cast off the mould and get at the living yeast imprisoned within it. At present many people are coerced unwillingly by custom and expediency to be part of communities they do not care about, and they lose a sense of the meaning of life. The task of the Church is to build a community with purpose forged from the Christian revelation, a community which is understanding, responding, so loving that people would sorrow to cut themselves off from it. Then, indeed, the Church will be built on rock, and the gates of hell shall not prevail against it.

Are there differences between the way the priest and the social worker look at behaviour? I think there are, but perhaps this is because each starts from different points along the line. There is first of all the difference about the fact of sin. To the caseworker sin is irrelevant in the context of his work. He knows and recognizes that certain things are morally wrong, irresponsible, and evil, but he looks at acts of behaviour this way—Why did this person feel he must do this, what did it mean to him, what lies behind it all? The casework method is designed to find this out. Sometimes, as in the case of the suddenly bereaved child who steals something of value to symbolize replacing the treasured mother he has lost, the act is seen as an appeal to compassion, a cry for help; sometimes it is an act of hate against a cruel world. The worker cannot change the behaviour except by giving to the child a repairing experience of love, either through himself or through providing some closer relationship. Sometimes actions are plain uncontrolled rage and self-indulgence. To the worker the causation and motivation are of importance as well as the act. What happened that the person never internalized control? No caseworker ever knows the struggle which goes on in a person's mind as he wrestles with "want" and "ought", how easy it was to come down on the right side, or how difficult. A Christian caseworker would say the struggle is something between a person and his God, so he could never talk meaningfully about other people's sins, only about his own. He is wary, also, about arousing too much guilt because he knows its paralysing effect and the serious depression that may follow it. He sees the genesis of guilt as fear of loss of the parents' love. Because he wants to be loved the young child imposes on himself the controls his parents require of him; if he fails he is afraid they will not love him and he feels guilt. This feeling persists through adult life. So excessive guilt is seen sometimes as a residual of conditional love; the person feels he will never be loved fully because he is not good enough. So he feels unworthy all the time. Since all human love, even at its most perfect, at times falls short of the unconditional quality, we all experience some residual of guilt built into our personalities. The social worker tries to strengthen the person first by acceptance, so that he feels that concern for him is unconditional and he can then face himself and his problem. It is really another way of saying that unconditional love must come before any sort of growth. So the priest can teach first the love of God; we realize then how immeasurably wonderful it is and fear to separate ourselves from it. Christianity is really ego-supportive. It is more than loving God and one's neighbour, it is seeing life in a new way delivered from bondage into a splendour which is the Kingdom of Heaven on earth.

To act as though we see life in a new way, as Christ did, is to be aggressive about the coming of the Kingdom of Heaven on earth.[1] To use aggression creatively as a normal, constructive part of our personalities is good. Often the caseworker has to change the wrong use of aggression into a better use, channelling it into fresh thinking, or into the client's desire to get to grips with his problem, get his teeth into it (notice how aggressive are the words we use to describe what is done), or towards the assertion of his own unique personality. The caseworker sees aggression as necessary, provided it is used in this way, enabling the expression of our potentialities,

---

[1] Michel Quoist well describes this Christ-like aggression:

Lord, it's too late for you to be quiet, you have spoken too much; you have fought too much;

You were not sensible, you know, you exaggerated, it was bound to happen.

You called the better people a breed of vipers;

You told them that their hearts were black sepulchres with fine exteriors;

You kissed the decaying lepers;

You spoke fearlessly with unacceptable strangers;

You ate with notorious sinners, and you said that street-walkers would be the first in Paradise;

You got on well with the poor, the tramps, the crippled;

You belittled the religious regulations;

Your interpretation of the Law reduced it to one little commandment: to love.

Now they are avenging themselves.

They have taken steps against you; they have approached the authorities and action will follow.

"Prayers on the Way of the Cross, 1, Jesus is condemned to death", from *Prayers of Life*, Gill & Son, Dublin, 1965.

and itself able to be channelled into acts and thoughts for the good of individuals and society. Both priest and social worker need it, for by their respective callings they are committed in each generation to a disturbing new world. Social workers can provide a mediating experience in which a person may come to question what life is about, but the priest has the means to find the answer.

# Books for Further Study

## CHAPTER 1

Maurice Bruce, *The Coming of the Welfare State*, Batsford, 1961.

M. Penelope Hall and Ismene V. Howes, *The Church in Social Work*: a study of Moral Welfare Work undertaken by the Church of England, Routledge and Kegan Paul, 1965.

Kathleen Heasman, *Christians and Social Workers*, S.C.M., 1965.

Kathleen Jones, *The Compassionate Society*: Studies in Christian social thinking, S.P.C.K., 1966.

David C. Marsh, *The Future of the Welfare State*, Penguin, 1964.

Philip Rieff, *The Triumph of the Therapeutic: Uses of Faith after Freud*, Chatto & Windus, 1966.

William Temple, *Christianity and the Social Order*, Pelican, 1956.

Richard M. Titmuss, *Essays on the Welfare State*, Unwin University Books, 1960.

E. R. Wickham, *Encounter with Modern Society*, Lutterworth, 1964.

Eileen Younghusband, *Social Work and Social Change*, National Institute for Social Work Training, Allen and Unwin, 1964.

Church Information Office, *Current Problems in the Understanding of Personal Responsibility*: two bibliographies prepared by the Church Assembly Board for Social Responsibility, dealing with the exercise of responsibility in present-day society.

Birmingham Council of Christian Churches, *Responsibility in the Welfare State*: a study of relationship between the social services and the Churches in a city suburb.

## CHAPTER 2

D. V. Donnison, Valerie Chapman, and others, *Social Policy and Administration*, Allen and Unwin, 1965.

R. Dubos, *The Mirage of Health*, Allen and Unwin, 1960.

Penelope Hall, *The Social Services of Modern Britain*, Routledge and Kegan Paul, 1960.

Cherry Morris, *Social Casework in Great Britain*, Faber and Faber, 1954.

A. F. Young and E. T. Ashton, *British Social Work in the Nineteenth Century*, Routledge and Kegan Paul, 1963.

B.B.C., *The Social Workers*, 1965.

National Council of Social Service, *Public Social Services*, 1966.

National Institute for Social Work Training, *Introduction to a Social Worker*, Allen and Unwin, 1964.

Family Welfare Association, *Guide to the Social Services*, 1966.

## CHAPTER 3

Felix J. Biestek, *The Casework Relationship*, Allen and Unwin, 1961.

Evelyn Davison, *Social Casework*, Bailliere, Tyndall and Cox, 1965.

M. L. Ferard and N. K. Hunnybun, *The Caseworker's Use of Relationships*, Tavistock Press, 1962.

Annette Garrett, *Interviewing: its Principle and Method*, Family Service Association of America, 1962.

Jean S. Heywood, *An Introduction to Teaching Casework Skills*, Routledge and Kegan Paul, 1964.

Florence Hollis, *Social Casework: a Psycho-Social Therapy*, Random House, New York, 1964.

Irene Josselyn, *The Happy Child*, Random House, New York, 1955.

Helen Perlman, *Social Casework: a Problem Solving Process*, University of Chicago Press, 1957.

Karl and Elizabeth de Schweinitz, *Interviewing in the Social Services*, National Council of Social Service for the National Council for Training in Social Work, 1962.

J. Stone and J. Church, *Childhood and Adolescence*, Random House, New York, 1957.

Noel Timms, *Social Casework: Principles and Practice*, Routledge and Kegan Paul, 1964.

Charlotte Towle, *Common Human Needs*, American Association of Social Workers 1955.

D. W. Winnicott, *The Child, the Family and the Outside World*, Pelican, 1964.

Eileen Younghusband, *Social Work with Families*, Allen and Unwin, 1965.

## CHAPTER 4

Anna Freud, *Psycho Analysis for Teachers*, Allen and Unwin, 1931; *The Ego and the Mechanisms of Defence*, Hogarth Press, 1951.

Sigmund Freud, *An Outline of Psycho Analysis*, Hogarth Press, 1959.

H. Guntrip, *Psychology for Ministers and Social Workers*, Independent Press, 1953; *Personality and Human Interaction*, Hogarth Press, 1961.

Peter Hays, *New Horizons in Psychiatry*, Pelican, 1964.

Ernest Jones, *Life and Work of Sigmund Freud*, Pelican.

Earl A. Loomis, *The Self in Pilgrimage*, S.C.M. Press, 1961.

Melanie Klein, *Our Adult World and its Roots in Infancy and other Essays*, Heinemann, 1962; *Love, Hate and Reparation*, Hogarth Press, 1962.

Philip Rieff, *Freud: The Mind of the Moralist*, University Paperbacks, 1965.

David Stafford Clark, *Psychiatry Today*, Pelican, 1954; *What Freud Really Said*, Macdonald, 1965.

Anthony Storr, *The Integrity of the Personality*, Pelican.

## CHAPTER 5

Carmen Bernos de Grasztold, *Prayers from the Ark*, Macmillan, 1963.

Bruce Kenrick, *Come out of the Wilderness*, Fontana Books, 1965.

I. E. P. Menzies, *A Case Study in the Functioning of Social Systems as a Defence against Anxiety* (Human Relations, 1960, 13, No. 2).

Mary Morse, *The Unattached*, Pelican, 1965.

Helen U. Phillips, *Essentials of Social Group Work Skill*, Association Press, New York, 1957.

Michael Quoist, *Prayers of Life*, M. H. Gill, Dublin, 1963.

A. Raines, *Creative Brooding*, Macmillan, New York, 1966.

A. K. Rice, *Learning for Leadership—Interpersonal and Intergroup Relations*, Tavistock Publications, 1965.

L. J. Sherrill, *The Struggle of the Soul*, Collier-Macmillan, 1961.

Paul Tournier, *The Meaning of Persons*, S.C.M. Press, 1957.

H. A. Williams, *The True Wilderness*, Macmillan, 1965.


## SOME RELEVANT SOCIOLOGICAL TEXTS

Ronald Frankenberg, *Communities in Britain*, Pelican, 1966.

Leo Keeper, *Living in Towns*, Cresset Press, 1953.

Madeline Kerr, *The People of Ship Street*, Routledge and Kegan Paul, 1958.

John and Elizabeth Newson, *Patterns of Infant Care in an Urban Community*, Pelican, 1965.

John Spencer, *Stress and Release in an Urban Estate*, Tavistock Publication, 1964.

W. J. H. Sprott, *Human Groups*, Penguin, 1958.

Peter Townsend, *The Family Life of Old People*, Penguin, 1963.

P. Wilmott and M. Young, *Family and Class in a London Suburb*, Routledge and Kegan Paul, 1960.

M. Young and P. Wilmott, *Family and Kinship in East London*, Penguin, 1962.

National Council of Social Service, *The Caring Community*, 1966.

# Index